Canned Soup in a Walmart Parking Lot

By
Alex Bergland

Dedicated to my loving family and strangers with kind hearts

Special thanks to my mom for putting in so much time and
effort
into helping with the revision process.
I couldn't have done anything without you.

Table of Contents

Part I: Growing Up

Part II: A New Man

Part III: The Photographic Journey

Part I

Growing Up

1. Toto, I've A Feeling We're Not in Kansas Anymore

A big white van parked in front of a picnic table, a hammock strung up between two trees, and a dirty, drunk teenager crying into a can of green beans before noon on a Tuesday: I was a sight to see.

I thought I knew what it was like to be hungry. I had skipped meals and gone a whole day without eating before, but those hunger pains were nothing compared to what the last month had been.

I had made the decision to put gas in the tank instead of food in my stomach, I could not afford both. During the few weeks prior to arriving in Glacier, I started feeling the effects of that decision. By the time I came to the national park, it had been more than two weeks since I had what could be considered a meal. My daily nutrients consisted of one or two granola bars and water. Some days I had an apple or some other fruit, but usually it was just granola bars.

Despite the initial hunger, I kept going on strenuous hikes. I spent a couple weeks in the Canadian Rockies, and I was determined to see as much as I possibly could, which meant getting out in the mountains away from the roads.

I don't know if it was subconscious or not, but around the time I was in the Okanagan Valley, I started going on shorter hikes. Fifteen miles turned into ten, and ten turned into six. When I wasn't hiking, I was at a campsite or a pull-off on the side of the road where I could walk into the woods to set up a hammock to read or write.

The first full day in Glacier, I tried to hike the Lincoln Lake trail. The first part of the trail went through the lush, green forest that surrounds Lake McDonald. The trail was dirt and scattered pine needles. The going was not too steep, and the ground was soft and damp. It was a beautiful morning. I set my pace and breathed the clean air deeply.

Half a mile into the hike I felt dizzy and lightheaded. I tried to walk through it, but my vision started to blur. I stopped and leaned against a tree until I could see straight. For the first time, I stopped hiking because I physically needed to. After a minute of putting my weight on a tree, the dizziness went away. I shook it off, told myself I was fine, and kept going with a tinge of concern nagging at me. The forest seemed a little quieter, and my backpack felt a little heavier. The trail started to get steeper. I crossed a trickle of a stream and splashed the cold water on my face.

Less than a quarter mile later, I almost passed out. The dizziness came back in a rush, and my vision almost completely faded. I sat on a stump and put my face in my hands, fighting off the pressing blackness encroaching from the corner of my eyes. I needed longer to recover this time, and I didn't get back up for several minutes. I couldn't just shake it off. It would have been foolish to try. I was stubborn, but not stupid. Even so, the loudest voice in my head told me to keep walking and to not give up. It was only seven more miles one way. It was nothing. I knew I could make it there, even if I had to take breaks. But then the quieter voice told me I wouldn't have the strength for the return hike.

Turning around, going back, calling it quits . . . that was the last thing I wanted to do. I was afraid of giving up.

I had traveled almost 12,000 miles by myself. I had faced challenges and obstacles and had lived many incredible experiences. I was not ready to call it quits.

Not finishing the hike meant more than walking two miles instead of sixteen. It meant I had to stop running and face what I had been trying to put out of my mind for the last month: I was not going to be able to be able to finish my road trip in the way I had planned. I was broke and starving. I mean really broke, and really starving.

For the last week I had been strongly considering flying the carboard flag on the side of the road to beg for money, for food, for anything someone would be kind enough to give me. I was in Glacier National Park 1,400 miles from home. I had not eaten anything of substance in weeks. I had half a tank of gas and $43 to my name.

I had failed. Not just at the hike, but at what I set out to do . . . whatever that meant. I didn't start with a real itinerary, just a few places I wanted to go and some things I wanted to do. Along the way, I wanted to just see what happened. That was my goal when I first left home: to see what happened. Failure was the last thing I wanted, but there I was: sitting on a stump about to pass out from malnutrition. I couldn't run from it any longer.

I hated that I stood up, turned around, and started walking back down the trail. I hated that my pack felt lighter. I hated that I had realized I couldn't go on. I hated how much better I felt when I climbed into my van and drove back to my campsite.

For most of the trip, I had believed I was doing everything alone. Every choice was mine to make, every joy and struggle was mine to experience. If I needed something, I would make it happen. It was me with the world and me against the world, depending on the day. I had met people who had helped me and made the whole trip much better, and I was endlessly grateful to all those people. But at the end of the day, I was the one who had to figure out where to sleep at night. I was the one who found the showers when I needed to bathe. I was the one who drove thousands and thousands of miles without a passenger, and I was the one who found my way out of the woods when I got lost.

From the very beginning, I suspected I would become familiar with hunger in a way I never had been before. Throughout the trip, every time I went grocery shopping, I would buy an extra non-perishable can or bag of something and stash it away in a hard-to-get to place in the van and forget about it. Considering I had almost passed out from hunger and exhaustion only a couple hours ago and that my trip was nearing its end, I figured this was the right time to dig into my stash.

I lit a fire, pulled a can of green beans out from the storage space under my bed, and set it on the grate above the flames. I had nothing else to do today, and it wasn't like I was going to try to go on any more hikes. I poured half a bottle of gin into my cup and gulped at it while I waited for the beans to heat up. This is not how I pictured my cross-country road trip.

2. I Lost My Name

I convinced coach to let us go off the diving board after we cleaned up from the senior night swim meet, something we were normally not allowed to do.

I was co-captain of the swim team and a few months away from graduating high school. My 50-meter freestyle time was one-tenth of a second away from the state qualifying time. Up to this point in my senior year, life had been a rollercoaster of mental and physical health struggles coupled with insomnia. Swimming is what I sunk most of my energy into even though I didn't think I would pursue the sport further after graduating.

I wanted to do a double front flip. My teammates were egging me on, so I gave it a go. On the first attempt, I didn't rotate enough, and I landed on my back in the water.

"One more try!" I stubbornly said when coach and the lifeguards laughingly told me that was enough. I wanted to try once more. It was always one more.

I jumped higher, tucked harder, and opened up too late. I over rotated this time, and my feet caught on the calm water, which made my head whip that much harder into the pool.

One moment can change a life and can alter a direction forever. If I learned anything from the swim team, it was that one hundredth of a second can make a huge difference.

In that moment when my face met the water, I bruised my jaw, got a concussion, knocked several vertebrae into my spinal column, and tilted my skull off my spine. Of course, I did not know all this at the time. One moment was all it took for everything to fall apart.

I knew something was wrong as soon as I came up to the surface. From everyone's perspective, the dive just looked like a wicked belly flop. I could hear laughter as I swam to the wall of the pool and pulled myself out. I couldn't balance too well, and I was confused about where I was, what I was doing, and why people were laughing. I sat down on the bench built into the wall. Most people went into the shower room to shower and change into street clothes.

I had told someone I was going to a school event that evening, I remembered that. I got in my car and started driving to school. I had to stop at Taco Bell first. I was starving. I ate in the car on the way to my high school and somehow made it through the noise of Mr. CHS, our male beauty pageant to raise money for show choir.

The slight headache that started off as a gentle stream flash-flooded and become a raging torrent by the time I made it home. I stumbled out of my car, steered myself away from the stairs to the front door, and laid on the picnic table on our back patio. I stared at the white stars in the black sky. The pinpoints of light were beautiful, so far removed from the struggles of human life.

My mom eventually found me on the picnic table after looking for me. My car had come home, but I had not. With her help, I stumbled inside and sat down. A phone appeared in my hands, and I was talking to my grandparents. I had no clue what the conversation was about, or how I was responding. When I handed the phone back to my mom, her eyes were full of skepticism and laced with worry. She asked if I was okay. I said I didn't think I was, which was different from how I usually respond after an injury.

I told her I hit my head and was not feeling the best but that I would be fine in the morning. She wanted to take me to the hospital. I refused. I don't know if I slept that night. I don't know when I woke up. I drove the few miles to school, then drove across town to Missouri Western State University for a high school art show. I had a couple of ceramic pieces in the exhibition. What was I doing there? How did I get there? I wanted to go home. I wanted to throw up.

I must have stumbled into my ceramics teacher at some point in the early afternoon and told him I needed to go home. The last few months of sleep deprivation and the events of the previous day had stripped all the energy needed to maintain my "everything-is-okay" mask. I must have looked like absolute shit because it took no convincing to let me leave from the event. With concern, he told me to feel better. I shouldn't have driven home, but I did, and called my mom.

She appeared in the doorway not too long after. I do not know where I was or what I was doing, but the first thing she did was call and make an appointment to see the concussion specialist for the following day.

We found out that, yes, I appeared to have a slight concussion but would probably recover in a week or so. That was all we were told. Until then, the doctor's orders were to lie down in a dark room. I was not allowed to look at any light, listen to anything, or think of anything too hard. This was to be my routine for the week, and then, after that, I would resume school and likely be back to normal. Until I was cleared, I was excused from classes.

I laid in bed for the next few days. I could not do anything except for things that required no thought. Just about the only thing I could do was pet my cat who jumped into my bed to lay with me, purring and napping without a care in the world. At least she was happy I was home during the days.

The injury and doctor's orders lessened my worry of missing out on school, but I still hated being home. Regardless, I was finally able to get a little bit of sleep, just a few hours here and there, but still the most sleep I had gotten in the last couple months.

I was not too concerned about my brain. My previous concussions were minor, healed within a day. I thought this time would be similar and that I'd get to catch up on sleep and then return to the swim team, school, and to my business quickly. But that's not what happened.

Every day was like going down a steep metal slide in a dream as a small, scared child. Terrified of the speed and lack of control, I would turn around and try to grab onto the slide to stop or slow down. Sometimes I would stop myself, lessen my grip, then plummet downwards. The slide was too steep for me to climb or walk back up. I fell ever downwards. I could not see through tears; I lost sight of the ground. I cried out, but anyone who might have heard was unable to help. I was much too high off the ground. I continued the pattern of letting go, grabbing the sides, burning my hands, stopping. Still the ground did not appear. For every foot I fell, the slide grew by two.

Time lost its footing, and days blurred into each other. Each day was more or less the same. I did not leave the house much. Gradually, with the help of Unisom, I settled into a healthy sleep schedule.

For about a month, every day was just as bad if not worse than the day before. Sitting in bed made me stir crazy. Moving brought migraines. Thinking led to confusion. Being still was the best thing for me, but I had never been capable of being still for long. Instead of beginning mornings with coffee, protein shakes, and workouts, I began with migraines and blankets over my face to hide myself from the morning sun. Even temporarily untethered from responsibilities, headaches were constant, and there was not much I could physically accomplish.

Worse than the headaches was the mental fog that settled. My mind was heavily clouded. I could hardly trace distant silhouettes of ideas. Full sentences were illusive, and my thoughts became less and less coherent. Ideas became mist. Especially painful, one of the few things I knew was that I didn't used to be that way. I knew at one point I had been a smart, hard-working student and person. It is a devastating thing to know, that you are broken and have crumbled from who you were. It was like drowning. Occasionally I would break through the fog and see how unwell I was, and then the fog rolled back in. I stopped talking much.

It wasn't just my comprehension that suffered, but my memory as well. There were days when I had no idea what my name was. I carried my wallet with my ID in my back pocket even though I barely left the house so I could check what my name was, just to make sure I had it right.

I was angry and frustrated at what I had become. I had been a gifted student up to my chin in extra curriculars. I started, owned, and ran my own business as a freshman in high school. I had been capable and hard-working. I was a studious bookworm and didn't need to study before exams. I won competitions of all sorts. I was a multisport athlete. I had been doing much with my life, and I had been on track to do more. But sitting in my dark room, I cringed and covered my ears when someone ran the sink tap downstairs because the noise was too loud.

I have always been stubborn, and even though comprehension was difficult, at some fundamental level I was still me. I refused to sit still after the first week. I hated people who said I had to do nothing. I would not lie down and give up. I knew there were things that needed to be done and that the world was passing by without me in it.

My custom pen making business started to pick up around a week and a half into my injury. I received an increasing number of pen orders, and I did not turn any order down. October through New Year's was when business boomed. Customers wanted gifts for the holidays, and it was important to start the quarter with good numbers. So, I filled the orders.

I stood at my lathe in my parents' basement and turned pens for hours, even though the fog would grow dense after the first five minutes. If I was working in my woodshop, I could tolerate maybe 15 minutes of the light and noise before feeling my brain become a block full of rusty, dull kitchen knives. I took Tylenol before I started working which helped a little, but it was still a game of how much pain I could endure. I worked for hours at a time a couple days a week, barely aware of how much time passed. I tried to work at night to avoid the pain of daylight.

I had to learn my new limitations, and that took a couple weeks. Learning what I was capable of doing without causing myself even more agony was an arduous process. Cooking was how I spent most of my time. I learned how to cook when I was young and enjoyed it, but now cooking was just about all I could do without wanting to die by the end of the day. Cooking was simple and required little thought but still made me feel productive. My parents bought ingredients for whatever I wanted to cook, and I made enough for everyone. I loved cooking and spent most of my days in the kitchen. Cooking helped pass the time. Some recipes required hours of preparation, but time was all I had.

Being wrenched from my normal life pained me. I missed my swim team. I missed seeing my friends. I even missed my classes. A couple weeks into this new chapter of my life which I could see no escape from, I started going to school for partial days. I showed up to more important classes here and there but was never fully present for anything. I felt like a placeholder.

The school was against me. I do not mean the school made my brain hurt more, though it did. I do not mean that I felt far behind with no way to catch up, though that was also true. No, by saying the school was against me, I mean the administration was against me. I had been an active member of the school for more than three years, yet the administration would do little when I needed their help. The grades I had at the end of the semester, which was fast approaching, would be the grades I earned. As if I earned the constant pain I suffered when I was at school. As if I deserved to reach the end of the semester with a 16% in all my classes because I had just decided to stop showing up, lacking the desire to perform.

I was no special case, they told me. Students with cancer who had regular treatments and needed to be gone often were treated no differently, they said. What made me think I was so special that they should do something like unenroll me from classes I did not need to graduate so I wouldn't have to catch up on so much work? What gave me the audacity to presume the school administration cared about me?

The teachers, however, were amazing. They worked with me and allowed me to come in often after school to make up only the essential work and tests. They heard me and saw me as more than a student ID number. They worked with me and helped me keep my standing in the class. They had sympathy, even empathy for me in some cases, and because of them, I didn't have to drop out of school. I still had to work, and I frequently stayed after school to study or catch up on lessons, but, because of them, I wouldn't need to worry about dropping out. I am grateful for the amazing teachers who were there for me when I needed them.

In my foggy, agitated state I became angry with the doctors. After the second week, doctors stopped believing that I still hurt. They thought was I was trying to play hooky and that I had senioritis. X-rays, MRI's, and other tests came back clean. My results looked normal, which to them meant I was fine; I should go back to school and pick up where I left off. Appointments were scheduled in the mornings when I was most rested and clear-headed. The specialists did not see me the rest of the day when I was back in bed tensing up from a migraine or when I was walking around the house forgetting what I had just done and where I was going. I tried to function even though everything hurt. I pushed through because sitting still did not feel like an option. To doctors, I apparently appeared healed even though I was far from it. It felt like I got worse with each day.

I was gone for the whole last month of the swim season. My major goal of swimming at State that I had been working towards for the last two years was now taken away.

I asked mom to take me to the conference meet to watch my team compete. Being there hurt. All the noise and light. I had a knife in my skull for the hour sitting in the stands, but I wanted to be there for my team. As their co-captain, supporting the team was important to me, especially since I couldn't compete with them.

Word of my outing got back to the concussion people at the doctor's office, and they stopped believing I was still injured.

Around that time, about a month after the injury, Mom thought to try the chiropractic route. Maybe the problem could be in my neck, something the doctors hadn't checked. Doctors were telling me to go back to school full time and were annoyed when I protested. My mom took me to Hughes Chiropractic, and within ten minutes of the chiropractor feeling around and having me do different movements, he told me what was wrong and explained a possible route to take so I could start the healing process.

The main problem was that the top vertebrae were pinching my spinal column, so the nerve signals to my brain were largely cut off, which resulted in most of the problems I was having. The chiropractor snapped my neck, and by the time I walked out of the office, I felt closer to normal than I had for over a month. My brain was able to breathe after being strangled for so long. I cried when I got home. The heavy, dark fog that had settled in my mind seemed lighter, and I could see more of my surroundings. I felt hope. I remembered my name, and I felt sure in it.

I started to gain traction with my steps. The slide did not seem so steep, and though my hands were burned, they were able to stop me for a final time. I could turn around and start climbing back up. I was beginning to heal. With the constant support of my family, compassionate teachers, and chiropractors, I was on track to get my life back.

Staying after school several times a week trying to catch up with everything that I had missed, I made it through to winter break. The semester finally ended, and I finished with decent grades. I still had to go to the chiropractor at least once a week for many months. My neck had been out for so long that my muscles had reformed around my neck to hold it out of place. It would take a lot of time and work to reform the muscles.

Before the injury, I had applied to at least a dozen different universities and for lots of scholarships. I was going to study business administration and entrepreneurship, and I would be successful. After my world turned upside down, I couldn't bear to think about higher education. I was entirely burnt out from school and had not responded to letters from the universities I applied to. I didn't think I would go to college, at least not right away.

By January, I decided I would be taking the following year off to work and travel. I was thinking about maybe getting a van and building it out so I could live in it. At first the idea didn't seem too feasible. The more I talked about it, though, the more real it became.

I joined the tennis team again in the spring, had fun with all my teammates and enjoyed my last season. I goofed off in my last semester of classes. If you would have asked me in November if I thought I was going to graduate, I would not have been sure how to answer. For two months I was not sure if I would be able to finish high school. Then I graduated.

I said goodbye to friends, many of whom I may only see again at reunions in the future, if ever. I never had many close friends in high school. I was friends with a lot of people. but I did not belong to a friend group. I was always the extra. I had a couple of close friends, and I knew I would continue seeing them throughout my life. The goodbyes to school friends were not as hard for me as for others.

High school was over. Even though I had an idea of the direction I wanted to head, the feeling of what next left me dumbfounded. School was all I had known for my whole life, and I had been seeing mostly the same people almost every day for years.

Graduating is a confusing practice and is celebrated with more pomp and circumstance than it probably deserves. The arena floor was filled with students in the same mono-colored outfits. Energy and excitement electrified the air as each name was called and photos were taken. Then it was over. Everything we knew as students was over. We were nudged out the stadium doors into a world that most of us will struggle to navigate in. How will we spend our days? Where will we work? Will we go to college or join the workforce? Will we still keep in touch with our friends? Behind all the celebration, graduation is one big, lurking question of what's next, and most of us find ourselves speechless. The tutorial ends, and the real game starts.

During the first few months after graduating, I took some time off to recuperate. I was physically, emotionally, and spiritually drained from the year, and I needed to breathe before looking for a job. I needed a job soon, though. If I was going to live in a van within the year, I was going to need to start saving money, and fast.

I took a job at Menards in the building materials department and worked almost full-time hours every week. I sold lumber, shingles, concrete, sheds, drywall, insulation, steel, siding, anything you would need to build the shell of a building. Sales in the building materials department was a fun job. I learned about construction, how to estimate builds and repairs, and what materials were needed to complete a variety of projects. One week, the company had me working in a new store an hour away in North Kansas City building a post frame display for steel roofing and siding. I also got discounts on everything in the store, which came in handy when I needed new piece of equipment for my shop or needed material to do various renovations around my parents' house.

I worked there until just before Thanksgiving. Any Menards' employee scheduled for Black Friday who doesn't show, no longer has a job. My family gathers at my grandparents' farm in Illinois, eight hours away, for Thanksgiving. I wanted to see my family as much as I could because I don't get to see all of them very often. Family is important to me. Also, a day of greed right after a day when we are supposed to give thanks for what we have has never sat well with me. I wanted no part of working on Black Friday to support that part of our culture. I told my managers I wouldn't be work on Black Friday. They were surprisingly understanding even though that meant I was quitting.

During the fall after graduation, I also worked for United Way as a Loaned Executive during their campaign season. Being a Loaned Executive was not a paid gig, but it felt good to be a part of helping the community. I was responsible for helping to raise money for United Way to distribute among their partner agencies. I called businesses to ask for donations and spoke at company meetings. I talked about why they should donate to United Way and what good things United Way did with the money. The first presentation I gave alone was at 5:00 in the morning at a steel mill to about a hundred tired steel workers. It was an eye-opening job, a lot of work, and it was outside of my comfort zone. I learned and grew a lot because of it.

In the winter I went back to my seasonal job working Park Crew at Snow Creek in Weston, Missouri. The season started late that year because the weather didn't cooperate by staying cold long enough to blow enough snow to open. I had been working at snow creek for the past two years and snowboarding there for the past six. My job was to help build the park, maintain it, groom features, close things down, and make sure no one got injured in the park. If someone did get hurt, I would call ski patrol. The pay was not the best, but I got a steeply discounted season pass, which was the real reason to work there. The minimum wage paid for my gas to drive the 40 minutes each way to get there and back home to St. Joseph. At the same time, I also did a little training for ski patrol and became hill certified before the season ended.

On the Great Penmanship front, my startup business, I continued to turn pens as fast as I could and sell them at craft shows, online, and at Nesting Goods, a local home store in St. Joseph that carries products from local artisans. I filled increasing numbers of custom orders in the year after I graduated, better than the same month of any other year.

I was making as many pens as I could mostly out of the supply I had on hand since I did not want to spend more money ordering more materials. Non-stop production was tough, and it was hard to keep up because I had also been working at Menards, United Way and Snow Creek at the same time.

During the fall months of the gap year, I reapplied to colleges. This time around, I was much less sure about my desire to go back to school, and much less wishful to go to the farther-away schools or to aim for the bigger scholarships. I was still strongly considering studying business, though. I did not know what I wanted to do with the education, but business would be an easy degree that could allow me to enter virtually any sector of business and be an important check mark to have on my resume. I applied only to Millikin, Creighton, and Washington State, and only for the biggest scholarships available. I was a little greedy, sure, but I figured if I did not get a large scholarship, then I would just continue to make pens, work part time, and travel as much as I could afford. A degree didn't matter to me past checking a box on a job application. Continued education would be cool, but it wasn't worth going into crazy debt when I had no clue what I would use the degree for.

I heard back from Millikin first. I was accepted and was invited to apply for the full-tuition presidential scholarship and to attend the interview day on campus. Both of my parents had gone to Millikin and loved their time there. The university is where they met and where a lot of opportunities began for them. My dad even had the same scholarship I was applying to. My parents were the biggest reasons why I applied. Before I visited the school, filling out the application was mostly done to appease them.

I got to campus for the interview, and those two days on campus are why I decided to study at Millikin. The town the school is in, Decatur, Illinois, is far away from mountains and glaciers. The people are not very active. Harder drugs are abundant, and the city has a moderately high crime rate. Walking alone at night is a bad idea; that's what the students told me during the first night. Those things considered, the school makes living in that town worth it. Millikin is small, a population of maybe 2,000 students, so the education is more personal. Unlike a larger state school, there is more opportunity to do things differently, to forge one's own path. I would not have to be stuck in a mold.

I loved my visit, and the interview went well. A couple weeks later, I had a second phone interview, during which, I was sick. I was fighting the flu when the interviewers called. Somehow, I still made it through. The president called a week after the second interview and told me I had been awarded the full-tuition scholarship if I wanted to accept it, which I immediately did!

Just like that, I had a plan for what I was going to do with my life after I finished the road trip. I would go to

Millikin, double major in biology and business, and maybe even join the swim team!

The swim team dream was foolish, though. My neck was still weak, and every flip turn made it hurt more. During a summer swim league after I graduated high school, I could not make it halfway through a practice before needing to sit in a dark room and pray that the knife in my skull would soon be taken out.

Going to the chiropractor remained an almost religious practice through the year between high school and college.

3. The Shaggin' Wagon

The van was my grandparents' Dodge 2500.

I was looking into cheap used vans for a couple months before my grandparents offered to loan me the van they used to road trip in. They said they would fix the van up to ensure it ran well, and after that, it would be my responsibility. It had been sitting behind their house for several years.

We had to clean out some mouse crap from the back. All the fabric had a permanent moth ball smell. For an 18-year-old high school grad, the van was perfect. The van had already been converted to live in by my grandparents; the back had a platform for a queen size bed with storage underneath. Faded, maroon curtains covered the windows. Behind the driver's seat was a small dresser with a top that folded down into a desk. The space was not tall enough to stand in. There was only room to sit on the bed. In the few feet of floor between the bed and passenger seat, my head touched the ceiling when I stood on my knees.

The first thing I did after driving the van eight hours home from grandma and grandpa's was renovate the dresser. The back and bottom were falling apart, and chunks of wood splintered off. Once I tore the panels off, I found the frame was in rough shape, too. The paint was peeling, and some of the drawers needed to be fought with before they would open. The desk needed to be reinforced. Thankfully I was a woodworker and had all the tools to do what needed to be done well.

In our basement, I gutted most of the dresser, leaving only the top and most of the drawers intact. I replaced the frame with pine boards and bought birch plywood for the new back and side panels. Most everything went surprisingly according to plan; even the drawers did not give me that much of a fight when I redid the slides and replaced the tattered drawer bottoms. On the top part of the dresser that folded down into a desk, I added arms that would angle into supporting studs to the exterior of the dresser so I could put weight on the desk without the hinges tearing out of the dry wood. The finished product was sturdy and functional. Only finishing touches were needed

I found a cool travel-themed fabric to line the drawers. Then, I sanded everything down and painted the dresser white with black trim. It looked sleek, and I was proud of my work. The final step was to install eye bolts into its frame, bring it back out to the van, and find a way to secure it against the van wall so it would not shift or fall while driving down a rough road.

For the back doors of the van, I had another idea. I realized there was no place to cook, which was fine if I was going to pay for a campsite with a picnic table most nights, but I did not plan to. I wanted something that could slide out from underneath the bed so I could have a small area to put a small stove and plate on. Just a little countertop was all I needed. I bought sliders for desk drawers and installed them into the floor of the van underneath the middle of the bed. Next I attached the second part of the sliders to a ½" plywood. I attached a second piece of plywood to the first piece with hinges so when I pulled the counter out, it could fold out into a wider area that I could cook and eat on. It fit the Coleman stove I planned on using perfectly.

I wanted to replace the curtains since they were so faded and the curtain rods were bent, but I never got around to it. I did, however, put a tapestry up on the ceiling that stretched from the back of the van almost up to the seats in the front, so I had something rad to look at lying in bed. The tapestry pulled at the fabric on the ceiling, though, so I ended up attaching clips around the back of the seats and the sliding door to hold the tapestry up to prevent people from looking in through the front to see me sleeping. The fabric turned into a barrier that cut off most of the inside of the van from sight. In effect, the van became one small room that I could drive around.

I filled the van with everything I thought I would need for living for five months in weather between -20 and 110 degrees. The beginning of the trip would be cold since I intended to first head to the Rocky Mountains in March. I aimed to be in the Southwest in late spring. I packed two comforters, a pillow, clothes ranging from speedos and tank tops all the way to snow pants and snowboard boots. I was ready for everything.

I lashed a cooler to the back of the passenger's seat so I could have a sort of mini fridge. A picnic basket was stored underneath the bed full of food utensils and other miscellaneous cooking things. I had plenty of van maintenance tools and fluids, along with a spare tire. I had a trash bin between the two front seats. My dresser was full of clothes, books, journals, and toiletries. Half a dozen hoodies lined the edges of the bed platform that the mattress pad did not cover. In the back, I also found room for my longboard. I had a backpacking pack full of outdoor essentials like a sleeping bag, tent, mattress pad, water purifiers, a multi-purpose entrenching tool, some knives, a hatchet, and a thermal blanket.

One of the last van purchases I made was a pocket pussy. I didn't know if I would use it or not, but I knew I would be lonely, and it could come in handy. I also figured if I didn't use the pussy, I could hide cash there. I wanted to try and keep a couple hundred in cash on me for emergencies, and a pocket pussy is better and cheaper than a safe. There is no one, not a single soul, who would break into the van and put their hand inside my pocket pussy.

After purchasing all the van life essentials, I started looking into digital cameras. On Craigslist I found a deal on a Canon 60D with an 18-135mm lens. Future Alex could look back and reminisce about the travels in my life from the images I captured. I asked around for tips from a couple photographer friends and started to learn how to shoot in manual and about ISO, shutter speed, aperture, white balance, and all that other fancy photography jargon.

In addition to giving me something to learn while traveling, I found great value in learning photography because of its potential to be a memory aide. Even though I had found ways to strengthen my neck and I could go weeks between chiropractic visits, the spinal injury was one of those injuries that will never totally heal. My vertebrae still easily slid out of place and put pressure on my spinal column, choking my brain. When it slipped out, headaches, personality changes, brain fog, and memory difficulty arose. By shooting a lot of photos, I hoped I would be able to recall all the events around the photo when looking at it, and the image would hopefully spur memory hidden behind a cloudy veil in a hidden part of my mind.

The artistic potential of photography was a huge attraction to photography in addition to being a memory aide. I am not good at 2D art; I cannot draw to save my life. My art expertise is in the functional 3D realm. I wanted to learn a 2D art, but drawing and painting are very time consuming. All the drawings I had ever done turned out poorly. I didn't think I had the patience or aptitude for 2D. Photography, however, was a 2D art I felt I could do and enjoy, and the gear didn't take up that much space. Before I left, I picked up a 70-300mm and a 50mm lens in addition to the Canon 60D body and an 18-135mm lens. I could learn several different types of photography with that setup.

An old swim team friend graciously donated the mattress pad he used for one year in his apartment during college, and I laid that over an old mattress pad my grandparents had in the van. Honestly, the bed in my van was more comfortable than my normal bed. Although, my normal bed in my parents' house was more fun.

At home, my bed was two twin beds pushed together to form one king size comfort machine. I used to share a room with my brother, and when he moved out, the first thing I did was push the two beds together. Sleeping was not always smooth sailing on my two twin beds. A couple times I woke up in the crack between the two mattresses and had to wiggle and twist my way out like a half-asleep worm. One time I even woke up completely trapped, basically underneath the beds. I could not move, and I had to shout for my parents very early in the morning. Getting me unstuck took some time, not because it was difficult for them, but because they had to get the camera, laugh, and savor the "I told you so" moment of me trapped on the floor, pinned by beds and squirming around in my underwear at three in the morning.

The van slowly turned into my new home, but I wasn't sure how to feel about it. Looking out the kitchen window in my parents' home and seeing where I would be living for a while was exciting. Thinking of all the amazing destinations I would go to, the beautiful things I would see, the stories I could tell, and the amazing people I would meet made my heart race with possibility. At the same time, the thoughts were terrifying. I had never been on my own for an extended period of time before or been away from my parents for long. Soon I would be over a thousand miles away, trying to find parking lots to sleep in. No one would cook or clean or buy groceries for me. I had no job. I knew it would get lonely.

Some days, the upcoming departure, everything I had been preparing for, felt unreal. I was scared I would not be able to follow through and end up stranded somewhere far away with no one I knew even relatively close. I could be a 19-year-old far from home, sleeping in a broken-down van with nowhere to go. I felt comfortable enough with my skills that I could find some way to get out of most bad situations and be okay. Some things, though, I could not run away from. Being lonely for months on end, always going to the next place and never establishing friendships or seeing close friends were things I would have to face head on. I would be alone and drive thousands of miles by myself. How would I manage that for so long?

The traveling was not too scary a thought, though I was new to the solo travel thing. Growing up, my brother, Seth, and I were taken on several vacations all around the country and abroad, so I suppose I was as prepared as any kid could be at this point. My dad took us all around the world. We would go on month-long road trips to different parts of the country and do long drives before sleeping in a tent, the car, or sometimes a hotel. We would hike during the day and camp somewhere at night. When we got old enough, my dad would sit my brother and I down with an atlas and ask where we wanted to go and what we wanted to see. He would give suggestions about the area and answer any questions about the geography or history. Dad always seemed excited about traveling.

Energetically showing my brother and me the world is something I have not thanked my dad for enough. He not only showed us but taught us about the world. He made us get up early, do long hikes, and got us comfortable being uncomfortable. He made my brother and me independent and strong children of the world. Through him we learned how to navigate the mountains and city streets and all the places in between. We learned how to persevere because he did not give us the option to quit. We learned how to truly appreciate the beauty of this world. I cannot begin to imagine who I would be without him. My father instilled in me passion for the outdoors, which will forever be a huge part of my life and was the reason I believed I would be able to go on this van trip and come out the other side a stronger person.

To be totally fair, he's not perfect. Feeding my brother "energy pills" (Sprees) when my brother complained of being tired in Arches National Park, which led to Seth throwing up was one memorable flop. Another incident happened in the Rocky Mountains when he made me eat almost an entire package of hotdogs because it was bear country and without a way to keep them cool, we needed to eat them before they spoiled. Naturally, this led to me throwing up hot dogs in the tent at 3:00 in the morning. Now that I think of it, a fair number of his sub-par decisions resulted in one of us boys throwing up. He was not excluded from that trend either. One time he found an ancient protein brownie bar in his closet, packed it as a snack for a trip, and ate it while standing in line at a theme park. He regretted it.

Both of my parents were incredibly supportive of my goal to travel the country. It took my dad a little bit to come around, though. He had been gently trying to nudge the idea of college into my head for the first portion of my gap year, but when I settled on Millikin and started preparing for the journey, he could not help but get excited. My mom, on the other hand, was all for it from day one when I suggested the trip as a possibility. She knew leaving on my own was what I needed to do. She also made sure I packed things to be more comfortable that I otherwise would probably not have included. I think she hid some extra food under the bed for me the day before I left, too.

All told, I planned to spend about five months on the road. My travel route was only tentative. I would cut west through Colorado and Utah, then drop down into Arizona, over to San Diego, all the way up Highway 101 to Vancouver – with detours to the California National Parks that were in the interior – up to Jasper National Park in Alberta, travel down through the Canadian National Parks into Glacier, down to Yellowstone, east through the badlands and the Dakotas, then back up into Canada's Thunder Bay, around the northern side of Lake superior, down through Toronto, into Michigan, see family in Illinois, then back home to Northwestern Missouri. The route meant a lot of driving hours and around 10,000 miles, but I was as prepared as I could be.

March 5, 2017, that was the day I would go. Even if I was not totally ready for it or had second thoughts, that was the date I would leave. I didn't think anyone could ever be fully mentally prepared for something like this itinerary fresh out of high school. The urge to say "not yet" was strong for the month leading up to the date, and I felt largely unprepared to begin the journey even by the time I started driving west after doing the final check. I had the gear I needed, but as far as money was concerned, I would be in trouble. Before I left, I sat down and looked seriously at the numbers and ran through them a few times to make sure I had not gotten anything wrong.

Factoring miles per gallon, cost per gallon (estimating 20 cents above the current price), the distance I thought I would travel, and oil changes every 3,000 miles, I would need about $3,600 just for gas and oil. Of course, I would also need food, camping, park passes, possibly additional gear/tools, van maintenance, tolls, etc. When I ran the numbers, I had roughly $2,800 between my checking, savings, and cash. I hoped pen sales and perhaps the occasional odd job along the way would help offset the cost, but my hopes were slim. After doing the math four or five times and coming up with the same numbers every time I set the calculator down, and with a dopey grin, calmly explained all the complexities of my feelings on the matter to the walls around me. Fuck.

The last big thing I needed to do with the van before leaving was to test it out. It had been in the driveway for a long time, and I had seldom driven it around. A couple weeks before I planned to leave, I tested it for sleeping.

I figured a church parking lot on a weekday would be a good place to sleep, especially if I could park by church vans to blend in. So, one night I drove a few miles up the road until I came to a church with a massive parking lot and a few white vans the same model in the very back of the lot. It was around sunset when I parked back with the vans. I hadn't brought much to entertain myself in the way of books or my laptop. I did bring an edible though, and I ate a big brownie after settling into the bed to watch Netflix on my phone for a while. The edible started to hit me kind of hard, and it was starting to get late. I put my phone away and lay down.

Around midnight, I woke up with cold sweats at the peak of the high. The edible was a lot stronger than I thought it would be, and I felt sick. It was cold, and I was wearing only my boxers. I did not want to get out of bed, but I was not about to throw up in my bed. I threw open the side door and slid myself halfway out before I threw up all over the empty parking space next to me. After a few heaves, I slid the van door closed and fell back asleep half hanging off the mattress.

Sirens woke me up. It was early, and the sirens sounded close. I was so scared, and I still hadn't fully sobered up from the edible. I took a few deep breaths and got ready to face the cops, but when I pulled the curtains aside, I saw the fire department. They were farther away in the parking lot. They probably didn't even know I was there. I felt like I avoided a heart attack. I stayed in the spot another few hours to sober up and waited for the fire department to finish doing their drills and leave.

They were still there by the time I had sobered up, so I figured I should just leave. From the very far corner of the lot, I started driving towards the exit and had to drive around the three fire engines parked between me and the street. I drove slowly. The firemen did double-takes and gave me long and confused stares as I crossed the lot. All in all, I dubbed the first test a success.

4. Rocky Start

The morning of March 5, I woke up and almost convinced myself to push the departure date back another week. Almost.

I had excited nerves during breakfast, and I procrastinated leaving until the afternoon. I had not done much packing, so I had a lot to load up that afternoon.

I hugged my dad, mom, and brother goodbye at 4:00 in the afternoon. I climbed behind the wheel of the big white van and started up the driveway. I had driven up that driveway a thousand times before, but this time was different. Up until then, my parents' home had been my home and permanent residence. After I turned onto the street, that would never again be the case. It may still be my home, might always be a comfortable place for me, but once I turned the wheel, I no longer lived there. I would have to unpack and repack almost immediately upon my return at the end of this adventure to move into my college dorm a state away from the house now in my rearview mirror. After college, life would start.

It was a sobering 100-yard drive to the street.

Leaving something, someone, creates emptiness. It forms a pit in the stomach and tries to worm its way out of the throat, but it gets caught there. It can remain for hours. Making the left turn out of the driveway was difficult. Tears started to form, and it took all my courage to press the gas pedal down. The first step is always the hardest, as the saying goes.

I drove straight through Nebraska and didn't stop until I saw the mountains. Since I didn't have anyone to talk to, I had created several road trip playlists for different moods and different areas around the country. The first playlist I listened to was dominated by Matt and Kim. Any nerves or uncertainty I had about this new chapter were washed away as I screamed the lyrics to "Let's Go" and pounded the beat on the steering wheel.

My first destination was Fort Collins, where I planned to see my friend Jade. Driving time to Fort Collins was about nine hours, maybe a little more. It was late by the time I pulled into the parking lot of Jade's dorm, but some parts of campus were still open. We caught up a little bit over food, but we both wanted to go to bed because we had both had long days. I planned to be in town for a couple days, so we'd see each other again. I dropped her back off at her apartment.

Then it suddenly hit me. I did not know where I was going to sleep. In the van is the obvious smartass answer, but where would I park? As much as I had prepared the van, I had not done much research into van life. I had not read any blogs, watched any videos, or investigated much of what van life was. I had half-joked about sleeping in Walmart parking lots before I left, but suddenly that sounded like a good option. They had 24-hour bathrooms, any piece of gear I could want, and food. I drove to the closest Walmart and parked in a back lot by the automotive section tucked back by some trees.

I settled for the night around 10 p.m. and was hungry. Most of my foodstuff was accessible only from the back door, but it was 10 degrees with 40 mph winds at 10:00 at night. There was no way I would be getting out of the van for anything. I flipped the mattress up, twisted my arm into a storage compartment and grabbed the closest food item. I snatched my prize like a claw machine that works: a can of chicken and rice soup. In another part of the van, I found my can opener. Since eating utensils were only accessible from the back of the van, I had no spoon to eat the soup with.

If I could give one tip about how to be a dirtbag who drinks cold canned soup, it is to shake the can. Freezing in that parking lot, I cut my losses, lowered my standards, and put the bottom of the can to the sky. If the can is not shaken, all the substance of the soup settles to the bottom. The oil, salt, and juices will comprise the top inch and a half of the can. My first two mouthfuls were cold salted oil and chicken broth.

Full of gross cold soup, I climbed into bed, ready to be done with the first day. The wind howled all night and woke me up at several points. Whistling wind was not the worst part. The van was not insulated. When a big metal box sits in below freezing weather with high winds, it turns into a freezer, and the inside becomes colder than the outside. When a memory foam mattress is subjected to below freezing temperatures, it stiffens and becomes rock hard, trapping the cold inside it. I slept with three pairs of socks, tights, pajama pants, thick sweatpants, two long sleeve shirts, a hoodie, a coat, and a stocking cap underneath two comforters and two blankets. I was half-awake and shivering throughout the night.

I woke up in cold clothes on a frozen rock underneath a pile of cold blankets. My breath hung thick in the air, and the wind howled in the golden morning light. I stayed motionless in bed for three hours because I was too cold to move. The mattress pad frozen with a deep impression of my body; it was hard to roll out of. The growing need to pee finally roused me. I sat up, grabbed another coat, and slipped my boots on.

I never imagined myself being grateful for a Walmart bathroom, but that bathroom felt like a sauna. Until then, I'd never thought about how decadent brushing my teeth could feel.

Jade had class and then had to study all night, so I looked for my first solo hike. Jade recommended Horse Tooth. The wind had not calmed down much since the night before, so half the hike up was fighting the wind. The other half when the mountain blocked the wind was relaxing. I reached the peak, and everything hit me. I was doing it. I was out there alone, and I could climb mountains by myself. The hike took a few hours, and by the time I reached the van, my hands were about ready to fall off. The only gloves I had in the van were big snowboarding gloves, which I thought were unnecessary for a hike, so I didn't bring them. If I was going to do more hikes in the mountains in March, I needed better gloves. I drove to Old Town to find an outdoors store to get new gloves.

Warmth is what I needed that night, and a hot cup of tea screamed my name. One of the comforts of home that I brought with me was a tea pot that could plug into the van. When I got back to my Walmart parking space, I got out the tea pot and some tea, but the teapot didn't work. Another cold night was ahead. I downed another can of cold soup, shaken this time, and struggled through.

I was frozen, grumpy, and stiff when I woke up at 5:00, having barely slept. I thawed myself by breathing down my shirt. After the sun had risen, I got a text from Jade that made life better. It was national pancake day, and IHOP would be giving out free pancakes. A hot cup of coffee and free flap jacks saved my life.

I lazily tooled around the city the rest of the day and sat in a café for a while writing a blog post. I had set up a blog to record my travels and post photos for the road trip, and I wanted to update it every week or two. After I wrote the post and watched some YouTube videos on how to suture a wound if I were to get injured while hiking, I met up with Jade and we drove to Poudre Canyon. She showed me around her new home and took some amazing photos of me. She was the photographer friend who helped me out the most when I first got started with photography.

I left Fort Collins the next morning and drove down to Denver, where I had another friend, Jenny. I had a lot of friends in Colorado who I could visit for a few days at a time; that's why I wanted to go through Colorado first. This was important for my initial mental state. Couch surfing was a transition. Colorado would be at least two weeks of mixing my time between family, friends (some of whom I had not seen in at least a year) and myself. Going from being surrounded by people I knew to being totally alone would have been a little overwhelming, I think. This transitional state could help me build a healthier mindset before I moved on to states where I would be hundreds of miles from the closest person I knew.

I met Jenny at her dorm on the edge of the city. We got food, told stories, and at night we went up to Lookout Mountain for a view of Denver from above. The city was bright and seemed to stretch on forever into the horizon. Even from so high up, one could hardly tell where the city ended. It was just as cold and windy as it had been in Fort Collins, but we stayed for a while and smoked a bowl huddled behind a low stone wall.

In the morning I left to explore the city and suburbs. I looked for disc golf courses, but I ended up going to go to Red Rocks amphitheater and wandering around for most of the day. I found another Walmart parking lot to sleep in, and by then the crazy wind finally stopped. I managed to sleep through the entire night.

In the morning I met up with my snowboarding friend, Daniel. He showed me around the downtown Denver area, and we got burgers from a restaurant that supposedly had the best burgers in town. I think this place, City Grille, did have the best burgers, or they weren't far off. We hung around downtown for a while longer and reminisced about snowboarding days and high school. When we left, we went back to his school, and he showed me around campus. Then he let me shower in his apartment before leaving to find somewhere to sleep. I drank canned soup in a Walmart parking lot again and slept even more soundly.

In the morning I went into the mountains. I drove as high as the roads would take me. I was looking for a place to tent camp because I was feeling ballsy, but all the campgrounds were closed and covered with snow. I stumbled across a Boy Scout camp that must have had a couple year-long staff members. When I got out of the van to look at the lake, a very friendly dog ran up to me and loved on me for a while. I called him Rocky.

With no place to camp that high up, I descended. I had a full tank of gas, so I started making random turns. I went through steep canyons, followed the curves of clear, rushing mountain rivers, through small mountain towns, and was hugged by pine forests. I was lost, and I had no phone reception. I kept turning. I was free. I came to a sign for Longmont at one point, which was supposed to be my next destination, but not for a few more days. I had a great uncle living in Longmont who I planned on seeing.

A few years before, I spent a month of the summer working for him doing odd jobs like hauling dirt to make flat patches of ground, pulling weeds, planting, and trimming trees, and various other labors. At one point he wanted to teach me small engine repair (even though he is not a small engine mechanic), so had me bring old lawn mowers up to the garage to dismantle. After getting the motor broken down to all the bits and pieces, the hope was to put it back together. Neither of us had a good grasp on small engines, and we hadn't kept track of how the parts originally looked. Various engine parts lay scattered around the garage, and we had no idea what to do with them. It was a fun summer.

I wanted to do something before getting to Longmont. My phone had service again, and I found Rabbit Mountain open space. The park was clear of snow since it was more of a foothill than a mountain. I took my camera out and started wandering down the trail. A couple miles down the trail, it started to loop back. Where the trail ended was a rocky cliff dropping down to a plain below. I climbed down and followed a herd of deer around for a few hours before giving up.

This was the first hike I wandered with no purpose. The first couple hikes I wanted to hike, but this time, I was just wandering around and enjoying the scenery.

Crossing back over the five-string barbed wire fence, I caught my foot on the top wire, and fell. My camera was around my neck. I managed to get my hand underneath it as it fell onto rocky ground. My wrist took the brunt of my fall, but I saved the camera. It was only a sprain, but damn it, I had not even made it two weeks before I had to brace my wrist. I didn't think I was that accident prone.

I slept in a real bed that night at Uncle Plato's, and I stayed there for the next five nights. In the mornings, we woke up early. No, he woke me up early, and we went into town for breakfast to shoot the shit over eggs and coffee.

On one of the afternoons, I went to the rec center in Longmont for a swim. It had been a while since I had done laps, and I felt out of shape. I went, exercised, and swam. A blue diving board, poised and menacing, eyed me from the deep end of the pool. I loved diving and flipping. It had been over a year since the last time I had been on a diving board, and I still suffered those consequences.

I was scared, so I decided to conquer my fear. I climbed out of the water and stood at the beginning of the springboard. Looking down the board to the water was daunting. I ran, jumped, and before I could flip, my knees failed. I was airborne. The dive looked like a weak attempt at half flip, and I crashed into the water on my back. But I did it. I splashed in the pool like a happy duck when I came to the surface and got a few weird looks from the lifeguard. I beat my fear. I got out of the pool and did another few flips, real flips this time, and several dives. I found out how high I could get in the air and came down with big splashes.

At Uncle Plato's house was the first time I got my camera out and tried to take more serious, intentional photos. I put my 50mm f/1.8 lens on and wandered around his property at golden hour, finding a lot of things to take pictures of. This was my first time using this lens since buying it. I was told I should have a prime lens in my bag if I wanted to be a better photographer for various subjects, so kept it in my bag. I did not think I would use it for much after walking around for an hour trying to take photos with it. I did not like it, and the photos turned out nothing like what I saw in my head. I blamed the lens. A prime lens is locked at one distance. I did not think this was a very good idea, and it was a weird concept to me, so I went back to using my 18-135mm.

I helped Uncle Plato around the house and his yard for a few afternoons and prepared to head away from familiar people to start the solo part of my journey.

We shook hands on my last day there, and I drove into the mountains. The destination was Silverthorne, located in the middle of a handful of ski resorts. When I arrived, I sat down at a Vietnamese restaurant and had a bowl of Pho with a beer. There was a Walmart in Silverthorne, and that's where I slept.

The next morning, a friend from Snow Creek in Missouri, a ski patrol friend, stumbled across my van in the Walmart parking lot and said hi. The same morning, I got a text from one of my park crew friends who I had snowboarded with for the last few years. Soren and his family were going to be in Silverthorne on a ski trip later that day! Until then, I found a little trail out of town and walked until I got to an icy stream where I could set up a hammock and read for a few hours until Soren got to town. When he did, I met him and his family at a brewery, then followed him to the liquor store.

I dipped out and spent another night in Walmart. I wanted to ask to stay in their condo, but I didn't want to intrude.

I looked for hikes the next morning and came across Ten Mile. It went mostly out as opposed to up, which was welcome since the altitude had me out of breath after minimal exercise. Snow blanketed the trail, and I post-holed almost every other step. The hike was still beautiful; I think I made it four miles. On the third mile, I felt like doing something wild. I watched a lot of Naked and Afraid before leaving home. In this series, two people are dropped into a harsh environment, naked and with only the barest necessities to try and survive. My dad and I had a running joke about one day being on the show. I wanted to test if I could handle the cold without clothes for a short amount of time.

Beside a pine tree along the trail, I left all my clothes in a pile, except for my boots and a walking stick. I made it a quarter mile before turning back to fetch my clothes. I think I dropped one nut-cup size on that walk.

When I returned in the evening, Soren and his crew were back from the day at Keystone and invited me over for games and dinner. Soren's group kindly invited me to crash with them for a couple days while they were there, and I got to sleep on a warm floor without wearing a coat like I had been in the van. We went on hikes, drank, cooked, and had a merry time in the mountains for the next few days.

Before leaving Silverthorne, I sat at a picnic table in a park and pulled out my atlas. I traced the route that I had taken so far. Now that I had seen all my Colorado friends and family, I had no plans to see anyone or go anywhere. The lines I had drawn on the map seemed short. Though it felt like I was a long way from home, the length of the curvy black line over the interstates was surprisingly small. I looked ahead to the larger portion of the west and daydreamed about where I might end up. The journey had only just begun, even two weeks into the excursion. I had a long way to go. What I had done already seemed like a hill, and what lay ahead of me was a mountain. At this point though, I was not worried at all. I was already in the mountains surrounded by snow, and I loved it. From Silverthorne, should I cut south or stay west on I-70 into Utah?

Through the mountains, Salida was my next destination. En Route, I saw signs for natural hot springs with arrows pointing to the mountains, and I followed. The resort had two smaller pools at the location, but the real draw was the river. The spring emptied into the river of snowmelt, so the banks of the river was water nearing or exceeding 100 degrees. I could sit in the river and change the temperature to exactly what I wanted by building or tearing down stone walls that separated a pocket of the bank from the rest of the river. I stayed there until the resort closed.

I stayed in a hostel in Salida. I'm not sure why; the bed I had in the van was nicer than any hostel bed. I think I stayed because I missed having a kitchen and being able to cook. I had a Coleman stove that I had not used yet. Up until then, most of the meals I ate in the van were canned soup. The stove was too bulky to mess with, and I didn't want to tailgate a Walmart. I had brought the wrong cooking equipment.

I decided to give Tinder a shot while I was on the couch at the hostel. Why not, right? I was a man in a van down by the river, and even men in vans, especially men in vans, have needs. Meeting people felt doubly hard since I was never in one place very long, and I was too young to go to bars. Plus,

"Hey I live in a van. Do you want to see it?" is really not a good pickup line. So, Tinder it was.

A few swipes in, I had a match. My next stop was Grand Junction, several hours from Salida. My match was on the way. On the morning I left Salida, she sent me her address, and about noon I stopped by. We walked around the college campus she lived near before going back to her place and hooking up. I wasn't that attracted to her, but I was lonely and horny young man and craved physical touch. We had the house to ourselves, so we had a bit of fun before I got back in the van and drove towards Grand Junction. The sky was still bright blue.

5. Strangers

Coming down from the snow-capped peaks of the Rockies, I could see the entrance to the Southwest. The jagged peaks changed into flat mesas, and the ground turned from brown and green covered with snow to reddish-orange dirt and sandstone with many fewer trees. The closest National Park to I-70 is Arches, so that is where I headed first. I wanted to see all the nature that this country had to offer before we humans destroy the beautiful, natural part. Growing up, my parents took my brother and me to national parks, and it gave us an amazing appreciation of the natural beauty of this world. The focus of this trip was to hop between national parks with the occasional break to check out a city.

Highway 191 drops south from I-70 and runs through Moab between Arches and Canyonlands National Park. Traffic was backed up 10 miles north of the entrance to Arches since the park was doing road maintenance. I wanted to go to Arches, but I figured with that long of a line, the park wouldn't really be worth it, especially since I had been there before.

I had never been to Canyonlands before; that's one of the National Parks in Utah we skipped over growing up. There are three different sections of Canyonlands: Island in the Sky, The Needles, and The Maze. Since I was going north from Arches, I ended up at Island in the Sky. Canyonlands is an area unlike anything else I have seen. Picture a canyon a couple miles wide and hundreds of feet deep. Inside of this canyon is another canyon, maybe half a mile wide or more, and a couple hundred feet deep. Inside of this canyon is a narrow and not too deep canyon containing the Green River. At the highest points of the park on different sides lie the national park entrances. I drove to the very end of Island in the Sky and overlooked the scene of Russian Nesting Doll Canyons.

Sunset was still a couple hours off, but I got all my camera gear set up early on the edge of the canyon and waited. A couple other photographers were already there, and as I got set up, we shared small talk about camera gear. Finally, sunset came and bathed the sky with a brilliant yellow-orange horizon glow that bled into the light blue of the evening sky overhead and to the East.

When the sun had set, I realized I did not know where to sleep because within a National Park, sleeping in a parking lot is frowned upon. I turned around from the end of Island in the Sky Road and headed back to the campground I had passed earlier in the day. Every spot was full, and the sky was already dark.

One of the sites had a cardboard sign standing in front of the number which read, "We have extra room! Will trade a spot for alcohol/firewood." I had no firewood, but I did have a bottle of vodka. So, I parked and said hi to my new neighbors. I told them I brought vodka. They said the sign was mostly a joke, but if I was offering, they wouldn't turn down a drink. None of us had mixers, and we did not want to do shots. I remembered one of the food things Uncle Plato had sent with me was a box of Capri Sun. I pulled out a pouch for each of us.

The couple I shared the site with were young, traveling around the U.S. sleeping in campgrounds and hiking with their cat. Their cat, less than a year old, went on hikes with them and slept in a hammock at the campsite and in their tent at night. It was not until the woman mentioned a cat that I saw a tiny hammock hanging from one of their normal hammocks. A cat face was poking out, looking at me. I got excited, and the cat jumped out and let me pet her. I missed my cats back home, so I was so overjoyed to pet the little furball.

For the rest of the night, we sipped vodka Capri Sun, told jokes, and gave each other suggestions of things to see in different parts of the country. They had just started the travel life and had a lot of the world left to see. They told me how they had both left their jobs after a couple years of saving up money. They were both tired of the daily hassle of commuting to sit behind desks and hating their lives for eight hours a day, so they decided to leave it all behind to see the world.

The next morning, they packed up and left before I woke up.

I headed out of the park after having a slow morning eating a breakfast of cinnamon rolls and oatmeal with fruit. Since each edge of the park was small, most of the hikes were short, or little more than scenic pull-offs. One of the day hikes I did before afternoon was a route to peninsula that cut farther into the interior canyon.

For the first third of the hike, I was behind an older couple who were quite chatty, the man in particular. He would not shut up about my generation and how we are all glued to our phones and how he was so worried for the future because we are all lazy pieces of shit who do not know what work is. He rambled on, that we should just go outside and put our phones down and quit playing all those games because they are rotting our brains and how when he was younger, he was expected to work and learn life skills instead of texting.

I wanted to say something to him, but I did not know what to say or how I would say it. I wanted to interject to defend my generation, but I also felt like he was right. Eventually, the couple stopped to take a selfie at a very scenic part of the trail. I had my camera slung over my shoulders; I had decided that no matter what length of hike I was on, I would have my camera. I found it was an amazing tool to talk to people. At National Parks and monuments, almost everyone tries to take group or individual photos on vacations, and since I had a professional looking camera, I was often chosen, or I volunteered to take group or couple photos.

I asked the couple if they wanted me to take their photo. The man gave me a stink eye, but his wife was glad and handed me their camera. After I took their photo, I asked them where they were from, where they were going, and how long they had been traveling. The man either did not respond or only gave short answers when I asked him direct questions.

The wife, though, seemed lovely and was happy to chat as we walked down the trail.

After I fired questions at them, the woman asked a few questions about me: where I was from, where I was going, the same sorts of things. I told them where I had been so far and where I was planning to go. She asked my age, and they both looked surprised when I said 19.

The man started talking more and asked me smart-ass questions like if I missed my video games or if I was worried that I didn't have cell service out in the middle of nowhere, and what made me want to travel by myself. He seemed surprised that I was alone because of how codependent my generation is. He was physically stunned when I told him I had never owned a game station; he almost tripped. When I said I had only just gotten a phone for the first time a couple months earlier, so I was accustomed to not having service, his mouth hung open for a second. He nodded along when I explained that I wanted to see the world and there were not many people I could tolerate for this long in such close proximity, which is why I traveled alone.

Before we made it to the turnaround point in the hike, we were all talking like friends. I learned they were having problems with their son and his family. These grandparents had not seen their grandkids in a couple years, and the last many times they were together, the grandchildren were glued to their screens and would barely look at him, much less talk to him. Their father was no better and would not encourage the kids to experience life, barely looking up from his own phone. When the grandpa tried to have conversations with his grandchildren, they would barely glace up from their screens or put effort into responding to a question or statement.

I understood where the guy was coming from, and honestly, I felt bad for him. I feel bad for a lot of people who had to experience the explosion and rapid advance of technology at a rate incomparable to anything else they had experienced for most of their lives. It is so difficult to keep up with technology, and there is always something new, especially as an older person. The man had good intentions

41

and loved his family. He just could not understand why they were killing their spirits and personalities by being absorbed by screens, and this angered and scared him.

They were spending another day in Canyonlands before going to Arches, then going east towards home through Colorado. By the end of the trail, the man didn't seem as upset and seemed to have a little bit of hope for my generation. We shook hands back at the parking lot, wished each other safe travels, and went our separate ways. The man even told me he was happy to have met me.

I went further southwest after exiting the park. I slept at a scenic pull-off and woke up to the bright desert scenery. I continued down the road after a cup of burnt coffee. I had yet to make a good pot of cowboy coffee.

I came to a town a couple hours south of Salt Lake City. Three thousand miles had passed, and it was time to get an oil change. I found an oil and lube place in Sevier, Utah, and then I got back on the road heading south to Zion. I probably should have learned how to change my own oil; it would have saved me some money, and it would have given me something to do.

I entered the park and immediately wanted to leave. I was agitated at the never-ending line of traffic and hot weather, and I was starting to feel a little sick. Traffic was backed up through the entire park, and the temperature was much too hot for comfort sitting in a van, waiting for the car ahead to inch forward. Driving straight through the park took three hours.

I felt like I had been alone for a couple weeks at this point. I had not seen or talked to anyone I knew face to face. Even though I had some good conversations with strangers, they were still strangers, and I never felt at home or at ease. I was hundreds of miles from the closest person I knew. Desert and mountains reminded me that I was an alien to all the places I went. It was getting tough to live in the van.

Sometimes I would have conversations with myself while driving or sitting on the side of the road. I would talk about the weather, what I thought about life and death, political policies, favorite parks and states, the things I missed about home, the things I did not. The cup had been slowly filling since I left Longmont, and now the boiling water inside was threatening to overflow. I started thinking about turning around. I knew I did not have the money to complete even a little more than half of the journey and feed myself. I wanted to talk to people, and I had already been gone for almost a month. Was a month not long enough to say I had achieved my goal? Maybe it would be better to turn around after Zion. So much of me screamed no to those thoughts, but even so, the idea of quitting nagged at my mind.

I made it all the way through and exited the park without finding a single open parking spot, so I kept going down the highway until I found another road that went through the backcountry of the park. It had almost no traffic.

I was getting a little hungry, so I parked on a shoulder and got out to see what foodstuff I had readily available for a quick meal. Only wanting a little more than a snack, I did not find much that I was in the mood for. I needed to go grocery shopping. Looking around at the landscape got me thinking. What out there could I eat? Cacti, bushes, and other desert plants were all around. Fortunately, I had service, so I could look up some edible plants. Turns out, the petal cactus all around me was edible.

I took a lot of time skinning one petal I cut from a patch, getting all the spines out so they would not stick in my mouth. I ended up with a rectangular chunk of what felt like hard aloe vera. The plant had a strange texture. It was like biting into a goo covered cucumber with some crunch to it. It tasted almost citrusy and was very refreshing.

Slightly more rushed because I was hungry and had already done it once, I skinned another petal in half the time. Unfortunately, I did not do a good job or go deep enough past the skin. Two bites in, I had dozens of baby needles stuck in the roof of my mouth. I couldn't get the needles out of my mouth because they were too small for my fingers or tweezers, plus I couldn't see into my mouth to try and get them out. That was the last cactus I ate. I went back to the road going through Zion to try again for a parking place.

Eventually, I found a spot in the visitor's center parking lot. I hopped on a bus and got off at the Lower Emerald Pool trailhead. Along the way, a Canadian family stopped me because they saw my Vancouver shirt. We ended up finishing the hike together, and they told me a lot about some places in Alberta I should go to hike if I ever made it up that way. I started the day in a bad mood, but by the end of the hike and after talking to this lovely family, my spirits were lifted, even with a mouthful of cactus spines.

I went to get a campsite to find every spot already full. Rangers advised me to show up to the gate at 5:30 the next morning if I wanted a chance at a spot. The nearest Walmart was in a town an hour away, and when the sun started to set, I headed in that direction. It was a long drive, but I needed groceries anyway. And I liked sleeping with a bathroom nearby.

When the darkness settled over the country, it also settled on my mind; I still wanted to give up. It had not been easy to this point. I was tiring myself every day with hikes. Most nights had been cold, uncomfortable, lonely. I wasn't making real friends, and I didn't feel like I was doing anything significant with the journey. I had a Bible with me, found almost a dozen verses about dealing with loneliness, then prayed. It helped a little, but sleep was still an unsuccessful struggle.

At 4 a.m., I awoke for a quick breakfast of a couple handfuls of trail mix before driving back to Zion to wait in line for a campsite. I did not know if this would be my last park on the trip or not. I wanted to go home, but I wanted to stick it out too. I hated giving up, and this would be giving up only a fifth of the way through. Could I live with myself if I gave up now? Would I look back five, ten, twenty years from now and regret tucking my tail between my legs?

For most of the drive back into Zion, I was praying for God to send me a sign. Anything to tell me that I was meant to be doing this and I should stick it through. Anything to calm my anxious jitters and to make me feel like the path I was on was not the wrong one. Fitting that this occurred at Zion.

I was not feeling well when I pulled into the line for the campground at 5:40 a.m. and found myself 12 cars back from the front of the line. I did not feel social. Though we were all told to get there at 5:30, the campground didn't open for registration until 8 a.m. People waiting in line began to get out of their vehicles to make breakfast from the back of their vehicles or on the picnic tables nearby. A few people played catch or got out other yard games for something to do while we waited.

I read a little behind the wheel, but at 6:30 I got out and opened the back doors to make coffee. My van was now arranged in a way that made more sense for me. I was slowly learning how to live in a van and where things needed to be so I could easily access anything whenever I needed or wanted. The stove, pot, coffee, and picnic basket of utensils were in the back under the bed, on the sliding counter, so when I pulled out the counter, I was ready to start cooking.

The people behind and in front of me were playing frisbee, and after I cleaned up my coffee, I joined in and played for a while. I talked with the people behind me, two university students on vacation from Colorado University, Boulder.

After thirty minutes of chatting and frisbee, we decided to share a campsite that night because it would save money. I would not take up space they needed because I slept in the van. They could use the tent space. Sharing a site was also a good way to make friends.

After another almost two hours, we made it to the front of the line and were assigned a spot. We parked in the site and immediately split up to go to different parts of the park to hike.

I opted for Angel's Landing, the most popular hike in the park. The day was beautiful with only a few clouds overhead and in the 60's. The park was just as busy as the day before. Surveying was being done on the Angel's Landing Trail. So, the hike had turned into a line of people stretching almost to the peak. After the switchbacks, which comprised the first two thirds of the trail, the final half- mile ascent to the landing was a tight line going up. The trail is narrow, at some points only a foot or two wide with several hundred feet of vertical drops to the valley below on both sides.

I started the hike with a flannel but ended up shirtless with the flannel tied around my waist, my camera slung across my shoulders, bouncing against my torso with almost every step. The sheer number of people made some areas of the trail sketchier than they would have been otherwise, but as far as I know, everyone lived that day. I only stayed at the top long enough to eat a quick sandwich and take some pictures. There were far too many people and too much noise to really enjoy the experience.

At the bottom of the hike, I caught a bus to The Narrows. The Narrows is one of the bigger draws of the park. When the river is low, you can rent boots and waders to explore up the river. The trail is the river. You walk upstream for miles, turning from the main river to go into side canyons, some of which create their own water trail system of sorts. When I reached the start of the Narrows, the water was too high and the current too swift due to a recent increase in snow melt. Though I wanted to do the hike, I don't think I would've enjoyed it much. The water was frigid, and I didn't have boots or waders. I returned to camp.

In the site next to me was a veteran in his late forties or early fifties camping with his son. His son looked to be about around ten. The dad was clearly ex-military, still sporting a military crew haircut, camo fatigue pants, tan army boots, a grey army shirt. He had an air about him that said he was not to be messed with and would not tolerate bullshit. He did not look like the type of guy you could or would want to walk up to and start a friendly conversation with, and I tried to keep my distance.

I went to the camp bathroom. When I was walking back, my intimidating neighbor man was walking back from the water spigot outside the bathrooms, having filled up jugs of water. Since it was about a minute walk back to our sites and we had a similar pace, it would have been awkward to not at least say hi. So, I said hello and asked how his trip has been and how long he would be in the park.

We made it back to our sites and kept the conversation going. We talked about hikes we'd done at Zion, other trips we had been on, parts of the country we like and other countries we had been to. We told a few stories about adrenaline-filled experiences and some cool activities and foods to try in different parts of the world. He was well traveled and knew what he was talking about.

The conversation changed when, after a brief silence, he asked me how old I was. When I told him I was 19, he was taken aback. I must have looked older; the grime of not showering for several days might have aged me. Then he asked something that had been asked before, something I would be asked many more times over the course of the next few months. Why was I here? I was just a kid. Why was I out here all alone so far from home?

His question pulled me into myself, reminding me how I had felt like everything recently had been overwhelming me. I was just a kid out on the road, not knowing what I was doing or where I was going. I was just a kid out of my comfort zone. I felt like I needed to do everything on my own, and I didn't want any help. The trip was supposed to be about proving to myself that I could survive alone after needing so much help dealing with my injury the year before. I wanted to escape and see what I was capable of on my own. I wanted to prove I could live with this injury and not be controlled by it. Recently, it had felt like I was in over my head.

I did not have a ready answer for his question. His tone and attitude suggested that he clearly did not want a short, surface level answer. So, I told him why, all of it. I told him about going through some health issues in high school before being ripped out of life by a concussion and spinal injury. I told him about how hard it was recovering and how I could not even think of college or any other future at the time, how I needed to get out of my hometown and face something bigger to prove to myself that I could still overcome challenges. I told him about going around the country to dozens of national parks with my family and how that influenced the destinations on this trip. I told him how I had prepared for this trip, how it had been so far, where I thought I would go from here. I told him how hard it had been recently. All of it came out. He stood and listened.

After I finished, he stood silent for a little while before telling me his story. When he was my age and just graduated from high school, he had been a troublemaker and did not have direction, did not know where to go. His family was not close. He was largely on his own, so he joined the military early and served for a while. The discipline helped him immensely and helped him overcome a lot of challenges in his personal life. Several years before our conversation, he suffered a back injury at work and was left immobile in bed for months on end. He was told he would likely not be able to walk again. For years he had to watch his children grow up without his support while he was stuck in a bed. He hated himself and his situation. At times, he was almost ready to give up but was determined not to because of his children.

He underwent years of physical therapy and pain trying to walk. His recovery was slow, but eventually he was heathier than any of the doctors thought he could be. Not perfect, but miles ahead of where he used to be. He told me how hard that experience was and how he grew because of it. He talked about how much help he had along the way and how, every day, he felt indebted to the people who helped him.

I did not respond for a while, trying to absorb his story. Before I could say anything, he spoke again and said he knew where I was in life, how hard it can be, and what it felt like to be alone, thousands of miles from a friend. He said my parents loved me. It was not a question. He said they love me and must have helped me tremendously to get to this point and that I owe them a debt I can never repay.

He told me that the journey gets so much better and so much worse. He predicted that I had a long and winding road ahead and that, after this road trip, I would return as someone else: someone older, someone stronger. He told me what I was doing was a good thing to do, something that more people should attempt. He admired the fact that I was trying, even if it felt like I was failing, to seek answers to my life and to find my limits.

The last thing he told me was that he had a lot of help recovering and still needed help. It is impossible to get through this life without accepting help from others, he said, and it is the largest sin to not return that kindness to others.

I was dumbfounded. I had never had a conversation like this before, especially with a stranger or someone so much older than me. He called me a kid at first and then spoke to me like an adult. I was somewhere in between a boy and a man.

Our conversation marked a change. Instead of thinking of whether to go home the next day, I started thinking of who I was when I started and who I was now. I could see that I had already changed. The entirety of the road trip, the purpose behind it all, boiled down to a single, clear question. Who will I be when I return from the journey? If I went home after Zion, I would have had some cool memories, but what I would remember most is that I gave up when it got hard.

If I kept going, I would be consciously choosing to intentionally face even more hardships and uncomfortable situations. But had I not felt confident about making it through challenges before I left? I had to learn how to accept help, not only when I seek it, but when it is handed to me by a stranger. Would I do it? Would I repay kindness and assistance in kind to the next traveler I came across?

Our conversation cooled as I digested my neighbor's words and my thoughts. We talked a little more. Then he started a fire and began cooking for his son who was riding around the campground on a bike. We had talked for the better part of three hours, and the sun had set by the time our conversation closed.

By then, the two men who shared my site had returned from their day, and I helped them set up their tent in the fading light. I still had not eaten because of the unexpectedly long interaction with the man I had tried to avoid. Just outside the park was a small town with a Mexican restaurant. Both my campsite companions were keen to try it, and they invited me along.

We had some burritos and margheritas, then returned to the campsite for a fire to end the night. We sat around the fire and shared some of our stories. I told a shortened version of my story, still trying to process the earlier conversation. At the end of the night, the two said they were leaving the next day. They might not see me in the morning, as their classes were starting back up in two days, and they had a long drive to get back. One of them asked me if I was Christian, and I said that I thought so. He asked if he could pray for me. He was in school studying to become a youth minister and was almost ready to graduate. So, we prayed.

Morning brought rain and heavy grey clouds low over the valley. I had no desire to get up. I wanted, instead, to lie in bed and think all day. The sound of the camp next to mine being torn down roused me. I could not let the military man leave without saying thank you. I threw on some layers, dropped out of the van, and asked if he wanted coffee. I did not have much to share with others, but I figured I could always offer coffee or tea to someone.

He said he would love some coffee, and then I remembered that I did not know how to make coffee that could be enjoyed. I felt bad as I poured us each a cup. I could immediately tell that he was not a fan. The coffee was burned and way too strong. Once he sipped some, he filled the cup back up with creamer from his truck.

We talked a little more while he tore down, and once all his stuff was packed away, he turned back to me. I said thank you. He told me not to thank him. He was just an old man who had been through some shit and went on a camping trip with his son and talked with a stranger at the campground.

Before I could respond, he told me to let him give me something. He told me he was leaving all his food with me. I opened my mouth and barely managed to choke out that I was grateful, but . . . his eyes pierced mine. He told me I was going to let him help me and that I was not going to say anything to prevent it. I closed my mouth. I looked down, back up, and said thank you. He left me enough food for at least a dozen sandwiches with artisan meat, cheese, mustard, vegetables from a farmer's market, sausages, chips, pancake mix, syrup, and the coffee creamer.

Together, we closed my van packed with his food. He crossed is arms and told me that Karma has a way of getting back to everyone in the end. He said that both he and I had been the recipients of much generosity, that while we owed a debt we could never fully repay, it was our duty to try. If someone helps us up a wall, he said, we need to turn around and help the person behind us. We either all make it, or none of us makes it. We shook hands, and he wished me luck. I wished him the same and thanked him again. He set my mug down on the table between us, still half full of coffee.

Then he left. We never even learned each other's names. A stranger who I was intimidated by and was scared to speak to gave me some of the realest advice I have ever received.

Shortly after, the two sharing my site began packing up. I offered them hot drinks, and they graciously accepted tea. Once they had packed, we shook hands, and they, too, were gone. I was alone again, stuck between going back to bed or going on a hike. I was alone again. Stuck between deciding to go farther west or to go home.

With my dilemma unanswered, I started packing my bag for the Observation Point hike. I ended up at its trailhead with only a couple hikers around me. Observation Point was a much calmer, quieter trail than Angel's Landing. The hike up was strenuous with steep switchbacks. The first major section of switchbacks ended at the bottom of a canyon and the most beautiful part of the hike, but as I came out of the canyon and expected a view, I was greeted by a thick fog and low hanging clouds. Light snow and rain alternated for the remainder of the ascent. The peak greeted me with more clouds. The ordinarily incredible view from above Angel's Landing high above the valley and Virgin River was now white. Only white.

I ate a sandwich and started back down the trail. The clouds didn't look like they were going to lift anytime soon. Half a mile down from the peak, the clouds started to dissipate, revealing a moody green and orange valley with muted colors. Sometimes I had a view, and sometimes the clouds masked the valley.

Halfway down I came across hikers about my parents' age trying to take a group picture. I was quick to offer my services. The group consisted of three couples. They were grateful when I stopped and offered to take their picture. Afterwards, they offered to take a couple pictures of me with my camera. We said goodbye and then all started going down the trail in the same direction. I matched pace with them and struck up a conversation with the couple at the front of the line.

We joked a lot on the way down. They were a fun group of childhood friends who all had kids about to leave for their first semester of college. This was a celebratory vacation. They were about to be empty nesters!

Not too far into the conversation they asked how old I was. I gave them a sly smile and asked which ID they wanted to look at. This brought hoots of laughter. When they recovered, they asked if I was 18 or 19. I said 19, but also 26. The age difference brought another round of laughter. One of the men from the back of the group shouted up to Mike, the one who had initially asked my age, if he remembered his fake ID when he was a teenager. The third man laughed a belly laugh and asked if the one in question was ordered from the back of a High Times Magazine, had a huge pot leaf on the back, and a poorly cropped photo glued to the I.D., the one that said he was 23 when he was 16. A sheepish grin said yes. Then Mike defended himself by saying it worked at the bars when it was dark, and usually, he got away with it because it made the bouncers laugh.

The hike down was filled with more laughter and funny stories from dumb decisions we had made. We reached the trailhead, wished each other luck, and shook hands. Mike was the last to shake my hand, and in his hand was a folded bill. He grabbed my hand and held on for longer, gave me a wink, and told me to buy some beer tonight on them. We waved goodbye as they got into their car while I continued walking to the bus stop.

I went straight to the grocery store and bought a 12-pack sampler from a local brewery. A fire, cold beer, and a cooked sausage over an open flame was fuel for thought. I was going to leave the next morning, but which way was I going to go?

A few short hours away from Zion lies Bryce Canyon National Park. I was going to continue my journey and face whatever challenge came up until I was brought to my knees.

Bryce is famous for hoodoos and for being one of the darkest places in America because it is so far away from cities and towns of any size. The orange hoodoos were still covered in snow; winter had not yet lost its grip in the park. I reserved a campsite and went off to drive along the cliffs to stop at all the scenic overlooks.

I didn't plan on hiking. It was freezing. I was tired, and I didn't even have a bag packed. But I started walking down the Sunset Point Trail to take photos. I ended up going on a hike unprepared. I didn't even have a water bottle with me. I spent about two hours walking around the hoodoos and taking pictures. Then I wandered my way back up to the van and drove to the end of the road, stopping at every viewpoint before going to curl up in bed at my campsite for the evening.

The forecast was for a new moon, clear skies, and strong wind. Around midnight, I drove back to Sunset Point and set up my camera to do some astrophotography. The wind was vicious and occasionally shook the camera during exposures. I needed to take a lot of photos to get a few good shots.

While I was shooting the stars, a father and his young son came to the point to stare at the sky. The kid did not want to be there and was complaining about the cold very loudly, as if his dad didn't know it was cold. The dad wanted to see the stars and wanted his son to feel the vastness of the universe. The kid eventually realized his protest was falling on deaf ears and sat against the wall above the canyon, finally looked up at the sky, and was quiet.

It reminded me of my own childhood when my parents dragged me along all around the world and made me do things I did not want to do at the time. Now I was off in the world seeing more of it by myself because doing the things I didn't want to do gave me a better appreciation of the world's natural beauty.

That night rivaled the first few nights in Fort Collins, and I woke up feeling like a side of beef hanging in a freezer. I wanted coffee or anything that was warm. The wind was still gusting in the morning, which made boiling water hard.

After twenty minutes, the water still had not reached a boil, but it was hot. I put grounds in the water and waited a few minutes until I got tired of the cold and drained the coffee into a bottle. It was the best coffee I had made so far. Turns out, coffee can burn in boiling water.

I was sick of the cold. If I stayed another day, I would have been doing nothing but huddling in a nest of blankets all day, so I left the park and continued my route south.

I had seen many Instagram pictures of The Wave, which is a rock formation in northern Arizona accessible via a road off a highway in Utah. I did not know the road to The Wave was a long dirt path before I got there. Again, I had done little to no research before starting the trip. I learned as I went. Over prepare and under plan, that was the motto. That way anything that arises can be easily managed and enjoyed while still having that exciting feeling of last minute, unplanned adventure.

Rain from the night before had made the road more of a mudslide. In fact, the only other vehicles I saw on the way to the wave were Jeeps, ATVs, and dirt bikes. The other drivers gave me weird looks as I cruised by them in my passenger van. The road went up big hills and back down, seemingly getting muddier with each turn and hill. I made it to the highest point of the road after a couple miles of drifting through mud and narrowly avoiding getting stuck. The formation was still not in sight. Looking down the mountain, I could see the muddy road weaving further through the vast cream-colored stone landscape.

Turning around was my only real option unless I wanted to see if Triple A would come find me in the desert. I backtracked and made it to the highway. I didn't have cell service, so I just drove down the road to see where I would end up.

After seeing only three cars in the next three hours, a sign pointed to Lake Powell over 100 miles away. Lake Powell would be a good place to waste time. I had been to Lake Powell once before, but I was so young I don't remember much about it. I eventually saw a sign for a beach and figured I could spend a day or two on the lake. Since the warm season was just beginning, the temperatures of both the air and water were chilly.

I walked down to the beach to take a few photos of the lake. On the beach were a few other people looking out across the water and taking pictures, and there was also a group of eight people I guessed were in their mid-twenties. The latter were drinking and listening to loud music off to the side, away from everyone else. It looked like they were having an amazing time. I walked back to my van from the beach and traded my camera for a backpack full of beer.

Beer in hand, I sat down a short distance from the group where I could still hear their music clearly. Soon after I sat, a couple members of the party group came over to me to say hi. They invited me to join them in their day drinking escapade. It was early afternoon when I joined in, and we remained on the beach until midnight. We filled the day with drinking, music, running into the cold lake, and telling stories. I learned this later, but when I joined them, they were all peaking on acid and molly.

When we got tired of the dark beach, my new friends began to sober up and asked me where I was sleeping. When I told them I planned on passing out in the parking lot, they invited me to join them at their campsite. I followed them to the campground, and we sat around a fire to cook food and retox. A sweet potato was cooked in the coals. We shared snacks. Around three in the morning, I was the first to go to bed.

Before there was a hint of light in the sky, I woke up to pounding on the side of the van and my name being shouted. Slightly worried, still tipsy, and only in my underwear, I had one hand on a knife and cracked the curtain to look outside. I was met with a smiling face from one of the women who told me they were going down to the beach to watch the sun rise. I had slept maybe two hours, and the sun still had another hour before it would rise. Reluctantly, I slipped into pajamas and followed them down the hill to the beach. In the darkness, we sat on boulders near the shore and looked east. One of them had brought a frisbee, and while we waited for the sun to come up, a few of us played catch.

The sun slowly came up, changing the grey sky into a brilliant yellow that blurred into a bright blue, casting the canyon formations across from us into a deep silhouette. We basked in the light and new warmth. Exhausted from partying and staying up all night, we all went back to camp. They got ready for naps and found places to sleep. But I wanted to continue to my next stop: The Grand Canyon. We hugged goodbye and promised to keep in touch.

Since Zion, I barely felt lonely. People all around me had interesting stories, and I could have deep conversations with them. Beginning a conversation might be a little uncomfortable at first, but not as uncomfortable as being alone like I used to be. If I wanted to talk to a friend, I would strike up a conversation with a nearby stranger. We could become friends.

6. The Blizzard and the Sun Devil

Just over the Arizona border I stopped at Horseshoe Bend: the surprisingly popular view of a horseshoe shaped curve in the Colorado River. The parking lot at the pull-off was packed, and the trail to the viewpoint looked like a massive, wriggling worm of bodies. The annual migration of RV campers consisting of upper middle-aged and elderly couples was beginning. I only stayed an hour at Horseshoe Bend, just long enough to walk down the trail to the viewpoint to take a couple photos and climb some rocks. There were far too many people in a small area, which felt doubly weird when looking around at the vast emptiness in all other directions.

The road south followed along the canyon for some time before the main canyon split off from the road. Highway 89 cut through the desert and offered views of smaller canyons before the exit for Grand Canyon National Park.

I passed through the Grand Canyon gate a few hours before sunset and had a comfortable amount of time to look at a lot of the viewpoints, walk through the visitor center, and find a place to sleep in the back of the camp store parking lot.

Around sunset I heated some soup up in the parking lot, ate it, and read before falling asleep. Finally, I was no longer feeling the cactus needles stuck in the roof of my mouth from the petal cactus in Zion. My mouth had been swollen and prickly for about a week.

In the morning I woke up and walked to Bright Angel trailhead. I did not have a permit to camp at the bottom, and all the camping had been reserved months in advance anyway. I had to settle for a day hike to the edge of the most interior canyon and back. The first hour was full of people and mules going down the trail and backpackers coming up, having left early that morning to avoid the warmth of the sun cooking them in the canyon. After that earliest hour, the population thinned to more hikers than observers. At some point, I matched pace with a woman while trying to pass a group of slow-moving backpackers.

We said hi and chatted about the weather and our trips. We had a lively conversation almost all the way down to the inner canyon rim where we both decided to turn around. Clouds were starting to roll in. On the way up, we talked about life and some problems we've been dealing with. In conversation, we each pondered if we were road tripping to get away from something or to get to somewhere.

She was a new mom and had some job problems back home. Her mom was watching her baby because she needed to get away from everything and reset in nature. A lot of unexpected things were coming up, and she was stressed trying to deal with everything. Being outdoors and getting fresh air was how she was surviving.

Emerging from the canyon, we wished each other well and took pictures of each other with a view of the canyon in the background.

I ended up on a bench eating another can of soup. While I spooned out the chunky soup, I smelled myself. It wasn't pleasant. I hadn't showered for over a week, and I hadn't done laundry for a couple weeks. My clothes and I smelled like dirty feet.

Doing laundry and showering wasn't something I had thought about too much before leaving. I figured it would all just kind of work out, that I would shower wherever I could, even if that was in a Walmart sink. Lately I hadn't gone out of my way to look for showers at truck stops. I didn't care much because no one was around to complain about my stink.

The campground at the Grand Canyon had a shower hall and a laundry room, so I decided to spend my late afternoon there. When I put the clothes in the dryer, I took a shower. The warm water and clean smell of soap was borderline orgasmic. When I emerged from the shower, finally clean after so long, my skin was a different color. I did not realize my skin was so dirty; I just thought I was tan!

When I went into the shower, all was bright and warm. When I stepped out of the door to the shower room, I saw snow out the window. It seemed to be the beginning of a blizzard. The sky had been clear all day, and it had been warm enough to hike the Grand Canyon in thin hiking pants and a t-shirt. I had planned on leaving after my laundry was done. Even while looking out at the fat snowflakes coming down, I still thought I would go. I didn't think a blizzard in April could be that bad or put down more than two inches of snow, and I had driven in snow before.

I grabbed my laundry from the dryer, threw it into my bag and ran through the snowy lot to my van. I climbed behind the wheel, started it up, and drove back along the southern rim of the Grand Canyon until I could turn south on Highway 64. The snow continued on, but the roads weren't too bad. A lot of the snow was melting as soon as it touched the ground.

A few miles from the turn onto highway 180, though, the snow came down heavier, and it started piling up. I was beginning to feel a little uncomfortable driving in it. At the turn, I saw a gas station. The thought crossed my mind that it would be a good idea to sleep in the gas station parking lot and finish the drive in the morning if it was clear, but I thought the snow would let up soon.

Everything was white by the time the road started climbing into the mountains. I could hardly see ten feet in front of my van. The road was steep and winding. The adrenaline high lasted for the next couple hours.

Out of nowhere, a car appeared, stuck in the middle of the road. A guy was standing outside the car. When I saw him, I whipped the wheel around and went almost totally sideways. As I fishtailed, the desk of my dresser unlatched, and everything flew out and bounced around the van. I managed to bring it back around, but I couldn't stop because the hill was steep, and the snow was deep. If I stopped, I knew I would be joining the man stuck on the road.

After narrowly avoiding another wreck about a mile later, I was ready to stop driving for the day and hole up somewhere. My white knuckles held onto the wheel with a death grip. The road had no shoulder, and I figured if I stopped at one of the day picnic sites I passed, I would probably be stuck in the mud for at least a day.

I pressed on, squinting through snow to try and find tire tracks in the snow. I found none. I fishtailed and spun out several times when the road turned or when I gave a little too much gas.

The road curved suddenly. I was going a little faster than I should have. When I turned the wheel, the van slid sideways. The back wheels went off the road, and for a second the van skidded on its frame on the steep shoulder. Time slowed. I knew I was going to slide off the road into a ditch. I was preparing to wreck. I pressed down on the gas in a hopeless last attempt to save myself. Somehow, my tires caught, and I was rocked back onto the road. All my curtains were knocked down, and everything was everywhere.

I hardly breathed for the rest of the whiteout journey to Flagstaff. The snow began to let up as the city neared. When I turned off the highway, the road behind me was closed with a gate for oncoming traffic.

I pulled into the back of the first gas station I came to and was asleep before my head hit the pillow. I was fully clothed lying on top of a nest of clothes, curtains, blankets, and any other item that found its way into my bed from the excitement of the drive.

At least a dozen people had told me about Arizona State Route 89A, the road that goes through Sedona. Supposedly, it is the one of the most beautiful drives in the country. I had a lazy start to the day and spent most of the morning in a café somewhere in Flagstaff. I edited photos from the past week and updated my blog while I was there, sipping on the café's signature drink. It was afternoon before I found Route 89A and followed it out of town.

The construction was awful, but honestly, I didn't mind. The drive was breathtaking. The scenery was green and orange. The road wound up mountains and around canyons. It would be an easy thing to spend a couple days along that road, camping, hiking, or relaxing by the river.

Sedona is known for just about anything to do with the outdoors and more. Many go there for hiking, mountain biking, climbing, art, nature photography, and psychics. The main strip of Sedona, still Route 89A, is a tourist trap with a lot of psychics, spiritual healers, bars, restaurants, souvenir shops, and other shops of the sort. The town is surrounded by shrub trees, canyons, and rocks formations. I found a spot to park and walked up and down the strip a couple times, meandering in and out of shops. I got a beer from one of the bars off the main strip.

It was getting uncomfortably hot. The heat of Sedona was a huge shock to my body. The day before I was fighting through a blizzard, and now it was 90 degrees and sunny. I left Sedona after spending a couple hours in the town and got back on the highway to Phoenix, where the forecast called for 105-degree temperatures for the next couple days. I found somewhere off the highway to sleep. I threw all the blankets off my bed and slept naked with the windows open. I woke up several times throughout the night covered in sweat. The bed was soaked with sweat when I woke up. I had just washed my sheets.

In the morning I drove through Phoenix to see the skyline but spent most of the day in parks surrounding the city, reading and writing. The first day came and went, and I found a Walmart parking lot to sleep in.

The next day, I woke up early and drove to Camelback. While Camelback is a short hike, it is difficult in 100-degree temperatures. The trail mostly requires scrambling up slick boulders. Since the trail is so popular, the rocks are worn down and slick in many areas. Halfway up, I took a short break to put a new hole in my belt because my pants were falling down my waist.

When I left home, I was two belt holes away from the end. Now one and a half months into the trip, I had dropped three belt sizes. A combination of hiking almost every day and eating much less than I was used to meant I was losing a lot of fat and getting more tone, especially around the waist. For the most part, I was eating two meals a day, usually consisting of something bread based, like rolls or some other baked good, and a can of soup for dinner, maybe some trail mix or fruit in between. Every time I shopped for groceries; I bought a couple extra non-perishable items to hide away somewhere in the van that was difficult to get to in case of an emergency.

I was sitting on a rock, drilling a new belt hole with my pocket-knife, lost in thought, when I was startled by a shout of, "Hell Yeah!" I looked up to see a woman grinning at me. She told me congrats and high fived me. She sat next me and talked for a minute or two about achieving goals and losing weight. Then she got up, congratulated me again, and continued hiking. I didn't know how to take that, and I didn't tell her that the new hole wasn't necessarily a good thing. She seemed really stoked for me though, so I let her be stoked.

I sat there a little longer again lost in thought. I was seeing the beginning of a downhill trend in my health and diet.

I descended the mountain and drove to Gilbert, a southwest suburb of Phoenix. Gilbert has a large park with fountains, walking paths, fields for baseball and soccer, and basketball courts. I watched a couple games, walked around the ponds and fountains, and called my parents to catch them up on what I was doing and where I had been, something I did every other week or so.

While I was on the phone, a wedding was going on not too far away from me. The couple kissed at sunset. After watching the reception, disappointed that they did not have a barbeque with a lot of food, I called my cousin in San Diego, the next family member I would see on my trip.

I slept in the park. In the morning, I found a café called "Bergies Coffee" which I immediately sought out. I think all the Berglands have been called "Bergy" at some point in our lives, so I had to check that café out. They had a large outdoor seating area with lots of trees and different styles of tables and chairs scattered under the shade. I wrote a blog post there and downed several coffees while I sat and enjoyed being in the shade.

I walked around the neighborhood after the coffee and went into Flashback Antiques. I spent some time soaking in the air conditioning and talked with the people behind the counter for a while. I found a few old yard sticks and grabbed one. For the past several years, my mom had been complaining about not being able to find a yard stick anywhere, so I figured I would bring this one home for her.

While talking to the nice ladies behind the counter, I mentioned that I made pens and had some with me that I was trying to sell while travelling. They were interested, so I went back to the van and returned with my box of pens. They bought a few for themselves and for gifts, plus a few more to sell in the shop. They also let me fill up all my water containers from their tap because they were concerned it might be hard to find cold water living out of a van. Water was something else I hadn't considered much before leaving.

I had been swiping on Tinder since I got to Phoenix, and I matched with a student at Arizona State. She picked me up form a parking lot somewhere and showed me around the university's campus. We hiked "A" mountain, a butte on campus that overlooks the Sun Devil Stadium. Then she took me to a zoo in a park. We didn't go in the zoo, but we walked around it and climbed some large rock formations. One of them had, well it was not quite a cave, just a large indent in the rock where we could sit high above the desert floor. The formation looked west, and we waited for the sunset. We stayed there talking after the sunset. Then we slowly walked back to her car, and she took me back to my van.

I slept at another Walmart that night and ate another can of soup.

7. Somewhere East of Jesus

I crossed the border into California blasting air conditioning in my van and screaming along to one of my road trip playlists. It was hot. I was sweating. And I once again smelled like a foot.

I planned to explore Joshua Tree and other parts of southeast California for a couple days before getting to San Diego. I wanted nothing more than ice cream and a cold shower, but neither of those was available in the desert.

I turned off the interstate onto a road that led into Joshua Tree National Park. Between the interstate and the park entrance was a cluster of RVs in the desert that looked like an upscale RV shanty town.

Driving for several hours and wanting to stretch my legs, I pulled off onto the shoulder and grabbed my camera soon after I entered the park. It was past midday, and shadows were just starting to stretch on the ground. I took photos of cacti, flowers, different plants, a lizard, and then I jumped 20 feet into the air and stifled a scream. A rattlesnake was woken up by the shadow of my foot about to step on him, and we were both surprised. He rattled, and we both jumped back from each other to a safe distance and locked eyes. He rattled softly, and I slowly retreated to my van, trying to stop my heart from jumping out of my throat. I was inches away from stepping on him and hours away from a hospital.

I was finished for the day after that. I had enough excitement and needed to acclimate to the new environment, so I went back to the RV camp and found an empty spot. I napped and sat outside in the shade of the van, watching other RVs pull in and set up camp. When the sun started going down, a lot of people started walking past my van towards the road. Most of them carried chairs and beer. Not wanting to be left out, I grabbed a chair and beer and followed the people in front of me.

As it turns out, this cluster of campers was there for a gathering of people who lived and worked full time from RVs. I arrived on the first day of their four-day retreat. Everyone who brought chairs set up around a bonfire in front of the Host's RV for an introduction. There were about forty people in attendance, and we had to go around the circle and say our names, where we were from, and how long we had been living in a vehicle, the usual sort of thing. Some were older singles, some were middle aged couples, some were young, some had kids, some were clean, some were dirty, some lived this way by choice, and some were forced into RV life by circumstance. I had to contain my laughter when it was my turn because I had no idea what was going on. I had just showed up randomly.

After introductions, the fire was lit, s'more ingredients were handed around, and we could talk with our neighbors. The man beside me had a thick English accent. I started talking with him and asking questions about what he did and why he was here. He was skeptical of me, and after talking for a little bit, he told me I looked a little young to have a full-time job and live this way. I looked at him blankly and asked if that is what this whole thing was all about. He raised an eyebrow and asked why I was there. I told him I was driving by, saw a bunch of RVs parked in the desert, and thought this seemed like a fine place to sleep for the night. He laughed a loud belly laugh and said that I had crashed an RV retreat for old people.

When he recovered, he asked why I was here, specifically here, sitting around the fire if I had no idea what this event was. I told him I saw a lot of people walk by me with chairs and beer. I like sitting, and I like beer. I explained that I just followed people blindly to the host RV. More laughter. This time, it took him longer to recover. We shared stories about our lives, travel, and work well into the night.

Eventually, he and his wife left for bed, and I returned to my home. He told me to come by and visit his RV if I wanted to talk more. I really had to poop before bed, so I dug a hole by a bush behind my van.

In the morning, I went into the park to explore. I drove straight through quickly but made a lot of stops. I did not want to do any distance hikes because it was so hot, I had limited water, and I did not want to stink up my van anymore with sweaty man smell. I am also not a big fan of the desert to begin with. Of all climates, arid desert and desolate landscapes are my least favorite. The desert was still fascinating to see and learn about. There was so much more life in the park than I thought there would be, but I didn't want to stray too far from the road.

The furthest I got from the road was about half a mile off trail. I wanted to move my legs more, and in the distance was a pile of boulders out in the desert. Intrigued, I parked and walked to the pile. As I reached the boulders, I realized they were much larger than they looked from farther away. I felt like a kid climbing around on the boulders. No people were around. I could barely make out the road and the cars on it from the edge of the rock garden.

When I got to the top of the boulder pile, I discovered, as if resting on a pedestal, an SOG Seal Pup knife in its sheath. I picked it up, pulled the blade out, and looked around. No soul was to be seen, and I could not tell how long the knife had been sitting there. The blade was dull, and the front pocket of the sheath held an almost empty lighter. I looked around again. Figuring the knife had been left behind and now had no owner, I attached the sheath to my belt.

Continuing on, I saw the Cholla cactus fields, Joshua Trees, dry mountains, and desolate valleys. I went on a couple short hikes. It was evening by the time I returned to my spot at the RV retreat.

I ate a quick meal and went to find the guy I had talked to the previous night. When I got to the RV he had described, I knocked, and he came out with a glass of water. We sat in the shade of his awning and talked some more. I learned about what it was like to manage an international marketing company from an RV in the American Southwest until he went back inside to finish working. I went back to my van, dug another hole to poop in, and went to sleep.

The sun rose, and the ground became hot. I got back on the interstate and drove to San Diego to meet up with my cousin, well, my dad's cousin, whom I had not seen in several years. I didn't know him too well, and it had been many years since I last saw him. I arrived in the afternoon to Martin's abode and carried in my bags. I was going to sleep under a roof, and there was a bathroom down the hall. I felt like a king.

Once the bags were in my room, Martin and I leaned against the counters in his kitchen and fired questions at each other about who we were and what we did with this whole life thing. Martin is a bachelor, and has toys that any man would envy like jet skis, ATV's, surf boards, etc. He has not married or had kids, but he has worked his ass off and had a lot of fun along the way. He returned to San Diego not too long before I arrived from a ten-day dirt bike trip down to Cabo through Baja California with some of his friends. I think he looked forward to a younger male family member visiting for labor, drinking, and getting some of the toys of out his garage.

We went on a quick Costco run and stocked up with food for the next week. That first day was mostly talking about how the family has been and making food. I took a long shower, too. My God, how I needed a cold shower after spending so much time in the dry, dusty heat of the desert. It felt like I was in heaven. I emerged feeling cleaner than I had in weeks.

When I was out of the shower and settled in, Martin went over some options for the next week. He was wanting to get work done on a house in the mountains, and I could help him with that whenever I wanted. But I didn't have to. He wanted me to have fun and explore San Diego, too. I could check out the city and all the beaches if I wanted, and he could give me spot recommendations. We could go out to eat a few times at Mexican hole-in-the-wall restaurants with some of the best Mexican food ever, go to his girlfriend's place for Easter, and if we wanted, we might take the jet skis out to Arizona for some jet skiing on the Colorado River. Everything sounded fun.

Before leaving for the trip, I had known I would be in southern California around the time of the Coachella Valley Music and Arts Festival, a popular three-day long, outdoor, live music party. I figured, "Why not?" I shelled out the money for a ticket. The shipping dates for the order got messed up, though, so my money had been refunded along with a voucher for $250 as an apology. Before I had left home, I reordered my ticket and had it shipped to Martin's house where I hoped it would be waiting for me. When I got to Martin's, there were three envelopes: a folder with my admission wristband, a folder with the parking pass, and a small, handwritten envelope containing nothing but a second admission wristband.

I thought about selling the ticket because that would have been an excellent boost for my bank account, but first I called my brother. I told him I got him a free weekend pass for Coachella if he wanted to fly out to Los Angeles and join me for a weekend. He was stoked about it, and over the next couple days, he made all the arrangements to get off work and get a plane ticket to L.A. and bus to Coachella.

In the meantime, I had fun in San Diego. I helped Martin with the house in the mountains. We put in a stone floor in the kitchen, bathroom, and a couple other small areas of the house. It was hot and heavy work, but really cool seeing the progress coming along and learning how to lay a stone floor. The mountain house was a couple hours from Martin's house in San Diego, and the road wound through beautiful natural areas with lots of wildlife. I ended up working with Martin on the house for three or four days while in San Diego.

When I wasn't helping Martin, I was a beach bum. I went to Ocean Beach, Pacific Beach, Windansea, La Jolla, and Children's Beach. I did a mix of longboarding on the walkways, walking up and down the beach streets, drinking beer in the hot sand, swimming, and taking pictures.

On the evening I was at La Jolla, a very wealthy northern suburb of San Diego, I hiked up a hill and out to a viewpoint above the beach where I could watch the sun set. After snapping a few initial photos when I got there, I sat on a bench to look through some of the recent photos I had taken while waiting for the colors and clouds to change a little more.

As I sat on the bench atop the viewpoint, two women jogged up the trail. One sat next to me. She saw I had a camera and started asking me questions about what types of photography I had done and what I was doing in California. I told her about my travels and my goals with photography. I showed her a few photos from my camera and my phone. She seemed impressed and offered me a job as her photographer for a new project she was working on. She was one of those famous Instagram people with a couple million followers, but she did not follow anyone back. She seemed successful and had a very strong personality. I thought about it for a little while and told her I would get back to her. I wanted to continue road tripping, but the offer was tempting. San Diego would be a cool place to spend more time, but I had already made plans to go to Millikin University. She left.

I thought about the proposal all night and most of the next day before I declined her offer. I could get a cool job any time, but if I took that job, I wouldn't have a degree to fall back on. The tuition-free degree from Millikin was too good to pass up.

I met up with a guy about a Craigslist post camera lens. My 18-135 lens was giving me a lot of problems. The zoom was catching and getting stuck. Something had come loose internally and was rattling around, and the autofocus was broken. In northern San Diego, I found a post on Craigslist for a Tamron 17-270 f/ 3.5-5.6, one lens to do it all, making a lot of things easier for me. I was not aware, however, that the wider zoom range on a lens typically means photos will be of a lower quality. I was becoming heavily invested in photography and wanted to pursue quality instead of point-and-shoot vacation style photos. I bought the lens for a couple hundred dollars, thinking it would improve my photography. It was in very good shape and had no signs of wear.

Towards the end of my time in San Diego, Martin was ready to blow the dust off his jet skis and road trip into Arizona. We hitched a trailer to his truck and embarked for a small town along the Colorado River near Yuma. Martin had a friend with a house there who was gone, so we had a nice house near the river all to ourselves.

Stand-up jet skis have quite the learning curve. Starting on my knees, I slowly got a little more comfortable after bailing several times. Standing up was uncomfortable at first, and for most of the first day, I was often thrown off as soon as I gunned it. By the end of the first day, I was managing to stand up and make wide turns with relative ease. Martin, of course, was used to the skis and ran circles around me at high speeds the whole time. Bruised, battered, and sun fried, we called it a day. Back at the house from the roof, we watched the sunset and stars come out.

The next day I went out with something to prove. The lessons I had learned the day before had stuck, and it was not long into the second day before I was racing alongside Martin and making sharp, hard carves and 360's in the mostly flat water. There was still some daylight left when we pulled the skis out of the water and got them back onto the trailer to make the return trip. Martin stopped at a scalding hot spring off the side of the interstate. Even though we stopped for a dip, I didn't dip more than my legs in. The water was too hot for me to handle.

Martin invited me to celebrate Easter with him, his girlfriend, and her friends at someone's house in the hills in north San Diego. On Easter Sunday we passed through the neighborhood's gate and pulled into the driveway of one of the nicest houses I have ever set foot into. The house had an amazing view and was full of people who were all dressed up in expensive clothes with their faces pinned back. These people seemed to live life like it was a show.

Martin and I were the obvious outsiders, dressed in shorts and clean t-shirts. That is not to say we were kept at a distance or smirked at. Quite the opposite, in fact. The people invited us in and were friendly the whole while. I did not feel like they talked down to me, and I quickly found myself drinking wine and joking alongside them. It was fun to pretend, but I never once felt like I belonged there. We ate grilled lamb for dinner, scrumptious and cooked primarily by Martin.

After dinner I was introduced to the adult version of an Easter egg hunt. The owner of the house had purchased something like 60 airplane shooter bottles of various liquors and had hidden them around the small yard. After explaining the rules, which basically consisted of "find alcohol," the dozen people at the party picked through the yard, bushes, and flowers until all the booze was found.

After the Easter booze hunt and watching a woman throw up into the kitchen sink after she took a shot of tequila, I made my way outside and met some of the children of the people inside. They weren't children, though. I was the youngest of the group. A few guys and a few girls stood around a car, passing a blunt and talking about something or other that sounded like drama. I joined in the circle and learned their names, which I quickly forgot. They were a far cry from the type of people I had gotten used to. Their personalities were so different from any of my friends back home or from anyone I had met along the way to California. Like their parents, the air around them was saturated with privilege, drama, and complaints. Also like their parents, they welcomed me into their circle. But I got sick of the drama and went back inside to find Martin and a refill, not in that order.

The rest of the night after everyone got drunk was chill. People played music, sang, and gossiped about personal life and business. We were almost ready to call it a night, but Martin had been talking about one of the guest's Maserati the whole night and didn't want to leave until he sat in it. The car's owner, Martin, and I went outside to the car, sat in it, and pulled into the asphalt cul-de-sac. Between revs of the engine, the owner talked about why he bought it: his son told him to, "buy the fucking Maserati."

I sat in the back seat of the Maserati and had to fight the urge to laugh about how quickly life can change based on who you know. A couple weeks ago I was hungry, eating cactus from the side of the road in the desert, having not showered in a week, dirty, tired, and smelly. Now I was full of lamb and expensive wine, sitting on leather, feeling the revving of a twelve-cylinder Ferrari engine.

Not too long later, we drove back to Martin's girlfriend's house. The drive might have been ten minutes, or it could have been two hours. From the back seat it was all a blur. The lights from the lamps formed an orange tunnel that resembled jumping to light speed in a sci-fi film. At one point, I think we even went to plaid. We arrived safely, and I was given a bed to sleep in.

Only a couple days remained before I had to leave for Coachella. As the date approached, Martin told me about the Salton Sea and Slab City, which I knew nothing about. After watching a VICE documentary on it, I was convinced that I had to check it out on the way to Coachella!

Back in the 1950's, engineers messed up diverting the Colorado River, blowing out a side of the canyon and flooding a Southern California basin for two years. It became a hot spot for tourists and vacationers and was quickly marketed as an oasis. This did not last long though, as the salinity of the lake gradually increased to the point where no fish, including tilapia, could live in the lake. Millions of fish died, and their bones drifted to the shoreline. In addition, the lake was prone to property-destroying floods from farm run-off.

After the floods, most people abandoned ship and left. Property values plummeted to nothing; they could not give houses away. Some people stayed in the town of Niland and in a nearby desert where a military base had been in the Vietnam era. The only remnants of the military base are large concrete slabs, hence the name Slab City. Slab City became infamous as a place where laws do not exist. The population is made up of vagrants and people without traditional houses. The people live in RVs, vans, busses, or makeshift homes made from whatever materials they can find.

As rough as this place may sound, it's strangely welcoming. The people are notorious for being welcoming. So long as no one crosses anyone else, residents are for the most part happy to be there and to talk to one another and visitors. The place has even been featured in films such as *Into the Wild*. The two most notable places in Slab City are Salvation Mountain and East Jesus. Salvation Mountain is a man-made mountain of straw, plaster, paint, and other various materials, created almost singlehandedly by a man named Leonard Knight who dedicated his life to creating this massive, colorful testament to God. Scriptures and praises cover the entirety of the mountain, an above-ground spiderweb cave system, and the vehicles parked in front of them.

East Jesus is the other draw. It is an outdoor sculpture garden in Slab City near West Satan that is almost overflowing with some of the oddest sculptures ever made. The residents take the trash and other things that wind up in the desert and create sculptures large and small that range from a bowling lane that visitors can bowl on, a wall of anti-consumerism TV's, dolphin conspiracies, and more than I could have ever imagined.

I was speechless at everything I saw and the way the people in Slab City live. Stranger still, everyone I saw walking on the side of the road or sitting outside, smiled and waved at me as I drove by. When I stumbled upon East Jesus, I was thoroughly convinced I was on a different planet. I spent a couple hours wandering through the sculpture garden, stunned at the insanity of what people can come up with, briefly chatting with one of the locals about some of the sculptures.

My mind was blown from Slab City. I left more confused than when I had gone in.

I slowly made my way up the Salton Sea until I found a campground. I had to pick up my brother, Seth, at a bus station in Coachella the next morning at 5 a.m. I needed some sleep because the next day was also the first day of the Coachella festival. I tried to nap, but it was uncomfortably hot under the desert sun. Coachella was an hour away, and the bus station was a little further. I pulled out of the campsite and drove north through Coachella. I scoped out the venue and the town, and then found where we would be sleeping for the next few days: a Walmart was about two miles from the general parking lot for Coachella.

I napped at Walmart until I had to wake up to find the bus station and my brother.

It was still dark when I hugged Seth. We were both very tired, so we went back to Walmart to nap for another few hours. When we were ready for the day, we fueled up on Starbucks and drove to the parking lot 30 minutes before the gates opened to the field.

Since we had time to kill, we just hung out in the parking lot and talked with the people next to us. We ended up playing Slap the Bag with the people in the spot next to us. We showed up to the gates tipsy before 11 a.m. and got in. It was over 100 degrees, so most people did not show up until the sun started to set.

The music festival had two massive, open, outdoor main stages and one covered massive electronic tent. There were also a couple smaller open-air stages, a couple small covered stages, and two indoor stages. Additionally, the grounds hosted massive art sculptures shaped like weird unicorns and another made of thousands of small mirrors. Rows of tents with souvenirs, games, food, and drinks were along the sides and in the middle. A Ferris wheel towered over the entire scene, and a large, air-conditioned projection tent sat near the entrance. Until evening, the grounds were mostly open, lines were short, and the less popular artists performed. Many of these artists were still quite famous, but with the heat and lack of people, Seth and I were able to get close to the front while the sun was out.

We sobered up in the heat and had to refill our water at the water fountains several times throughout the day while we got cooked by the sun. We had a schedule of artists. At the beginning of each day, we marked out who we each we wanted to see and when. We stage hopped all day the first day and spent the evenings seeing the big names like Glass Animals, Lady Gaga, Future, Schoolboy Q, the Big Gigantic, Marshmello, Father John Misty, Kendrick Lamar, Bon Iver,

Lorde, Porter Robinson, Mac Miller, Bastille, Two Door Cinema Club, Hans Zimmer, Preservation Hall Jazz band, Childish Gambino, Alt-J, Radiohead, and J. Cole to name a few. It was a proper festival stacked with well-known artists across several stages. The festival was a weekend long, each day starting before noon and running until after midnight.

In the evenings we were at the mercy of the crowd moving from big stage to big stage, a stampede of thousands of intoxicated festival goers. Each time a performance ended, the crowd moved like a flooding river to the next stage. Somehow, Seth and I did not get trampled.

On the second night, someone climbed the mirror sculpture, and when he got to the top, he slipped, fell, and died. A bouncer was posted around the sculpture for the rest of the night to tackle anyone who tried to touch the art or take a selfie with it. Seth and I stood in front of the crowd by the mirror sculpture for a while watching people get tackled and shoved.

It was an incredible weekend. Each day we woke up in the Wal-Mart parking lot and then spent all day listening to amazing music and wandering the grounds. Most people there were stereotypical Coachella attendees: Instagram models coming to show off their outfits for likes, only attending for a couple hours each day when the weather was not too hot. But there were a lot of people who had saved for a long time to be there and who appreciated every moment, my brother and I among them.

The Monday after Coachella ended, Seth had a flight leaving from Los Angeles, so I drove him to the airport. We hugged, and then it was back to being on my own in a big world, far away from home and the people I grew up with. I was so glad Seth had come. Growing up, he was always the person I was closest with and had looked up to most. Being able to party with him for a few days out in the middle of the desert was good, and it felt cool to be able to show him that I was doing well and happy out on my own in the world.

Right after dropping Seth off, I went to Huntington Beach. One of my parents' good friends from college, Susan, lives in Huntington Beach. My mom had called Susan and told her about my trip, and Susan offered to host me for a couple days. I do not like sleeping in cities, especially massive ones like the cities in Southern California. Cities are not my scene. They are too loud, often have more parking restrictions, and are just too dirty for me. But having someone to stay with for a few days in a city is an entirely different thing. To be able to go to sleep with a roof over my head and talk to people I or my family know made some cities enjoyable.

Susan's house is close to the beach, and I took full advantage of that during my time with her and her family. I borrowed a boogie board and a wet suit and drove down to the beach the second morning I was there. The waves were much bigger than I was used to, not that I was used to the ocean at all. Up until now, I had only done a little swimming and playing close to shore with small ocean swells on clear days, never boogie boarded or surfed, and never really experienced true waves. At Huntington Beach, I quickly learned where I should be on the wave: in front of the crest.

I felt good on top of the wave for a couple seconds during my first attempt at boogie boarding, then quickly regretted it. When the wave breaks, slight pauses in forward motion happen, and the crest of the wave curls in. I was unaware of this until the wave broke beneath me and I kept going. The wave I was on must have been four or five feet tall, and I dropped hard in the sand on my face. The wave brought the rest of my body around into the hardest scorpion of my life. I had snowboarded for a long time, so I had experienced my share of scorpions, but this was the worst. My feet touched the back of my head, and the wave pushed me even further, flipping me the rest of the way over and battering me against the shore. I washed up like a beached whale, and it took a few minutes of lying on my face in the sand to recover.

I have this stubborn habit of persisting until I get what I'm trying right. I had learned how to snowboard by falling hundreds of times and needing a few trips to ski patrol and urgent clinics. I didn't think boogie boarding would be that much a of a challenge. It took another hour of falls until I felt comfortable enough riding the wave.

Afterwards I walked around the shops along the shore. The streets were uncrowded and calm then, not busy like it would be later in the week when the farmers market stands would stretch down a street and when the stores would feature sales. I came back for the market on one of my last days in Huntington Beach.

Susan suggested I look on Groupon to find good deals on activities in the area. We stayed up a while one night, spit balling ideas, until Susan found an almost half-price sale on Skydiving in Oceanside the next day. Oceanside is between Huntington Beach and San Diego, right on the coast. Oceanside seemed like the perfect place to go skydiving for the first time.

The next morning, I woke up, ate some food, then hopped in the van to go down to Oceanside. From what I have heard, most people start feeling anxious about skydiving the morning of their jump, but that was not the case with me. I was excited. I was almost shaking I was so stoked to jump out of the plane. The hour and a half drive only built the excitement. I pulled into the parking lot of GoJump Oceanside and walked into the office to sign my life away.

Once I signed everything, I met Ian, who I would be jumping tandem with. He was a super cool dude and gave me a good rundown of what to expect.

Other jumpers beside me on the ground were nervous. A couple were almost crying. One of the guys was clearly trying to look tough, but his expression looked more like he was trying to hold in a fart.

I was stoked. No fear at all. I was ready. I could do it. We filed into the plane. Ian and I were the first in, which meant we would be the last to leave. The plane took us up to 12,000 feet. The ground looked small from so high up. Looking down, the view was split: half ocean and half mountains.

The door opened, and the first pair dropped. The second pair slid up to the door and disappeared. With each drop, I got more excited, even when hearing the bloodcurdling screams of people who just jumped.

And then I was up. My legs were over the edge, and I felt the full force of the wind against me. All the excitement that had been growing that day vanished in an instant. I did not want to jump out of a perfectly good airplane. Where was the sense in that? It was a foolish idea, really. Sure, it sounded fun, but in reality, it just does not make any rational sense to jump out of a plane. I was about to piss myself. I was about to turn my head and tell Ian we should stay in the plane, but before I could, his hand was on top of my head, pulling it back. He yelled at me to keep my head back as he launched us out of the door and into nothing.

We fell, fast. I screamed profanity as we reached our maximum speed. I felt like I was having a heart attack. After the first eight seconds that felt like eight minutes, the fear of death turned into acceptance. It was much too late to turn back. If I was going to die with this jump, death would be fast, happen in one of the coolest ways possible, and be captured on a GoPro camera.

The excitement came back, along with a sense of freedom unlike anything I had ever experienced. I smiled so big my face hurt.

Ian opened the parachute, and then everything was quiet. The view no longer screamed past us. All was peaceful as we floated down. As I gathered my bearings, Ian told me to grab the handles of the parachute. I did. I made a couple small turns. Ian shouted at me to put it into a spiral, to pull one handle down and push the other up. I did that too, and we dropped much quicker, getting a 360-view of the land and sea. I switched up, spiraling us in the opposite direction. As the ground neared, Ian took control again. He set us down gently on the ground next to the everyone else who had jumped.

I had never felt so alive before. Driving back to Susan's, I felt like I was living a different life.

On one of the days I was in Huntington Beach, I decided to go into downtown Los Angeles. Without traffic, the drive might take something like 20 minutes, but with the infamous 405 traffic, the drive is closer to two hours. I started to feel sick on the drive there, the first time I had felt unwell on the trip. As I crawled through traffic, I felt worse and worse, so I shortened my exploration to driving down Sunset Boulevard and going up to the observatory to look over the city before turning around.

I stayed at Susan's for a couple more days and didn't do too much but sleep and wait to feel better. When I felt up to it again, I thanked Susan and her family for letting me stay and for everything they did for me. Then I headed inland to see the Sequoias.

8. Seeing Myself for the First Time

The transition from boyhood to manhood, from child to adult is different for everyone.

Some are jarred into manhood when they see a dead body for the first time. For others, joining the military, seeing the atrocities of war, and recognizing themselves as an actor in it spurs the change. For still more, the metamorphosis comes with landmark events such as driving, growing a beard, graduating, getting a real job, becoming a parent, gaining huge responsibility, or another significant and recognizable moment.

As for me, I became a man while taking a sink bath in a Wal-Mart bathroom in Central California at 7:20 a.m.

I looked into the mirror but didn't recognize myself. I saw something other than a boy. I looked into eyes that could belong to a stranger. I saw that I was no longer the same person I had been when I left Missouri, and I realized I would never be that person again. I was elated. I was terrified.

Throughout my life and especially over the last month or so, I developed an addiction to adventure and to the unordinary. I saw adventure in the eyes that stared back at me from the mirror. I saw wanderlust, strangers, and the ineffable beauty of the natural world. Oh, the joy it brought!

In the same pair of eyes I looked into, I also saw a wild, beautiful animal who had just been set free into the world. I saw schools and careers and normality as prisons for wild souls and a life of adventure as the only type of life truly worth living. I was not born so I could maybe take two weeks of vacation per year. I was not born to sit down and shut up. I was not born to be numb to the world. I was born so that I may live.

I saw myself, not as being defined by my opposite, but by being my self and my opposite at once. For most of my life, I was given tastes of both worlds: school and work in one hand, play and adventure in the other. I had been walking a line, and now I fully recognized my autonomy to be able to choose which I wanted more, and which I was willing to fight for. The professional world was the easy path, simple but soul-crushing to get a job and work my way up to whatever I wanted to be. Adventuring and making a path for myself was a far more difficult route, but the one that could satisfy me.

I stood amidst the impossibility of living two lives simultaneously. Prisoner and jailer. Wild and tame. I was going to go from living in a van with the world out my window to living in a brick building at a university to make getting a job easier. When I stared at myself in the mirror, it was the internal conflict of identity behind my features, not the change in my physical face, that made me recognize my manhood.

Eternal recurrence is the theory that everything that has ever happened and ever will happen is destined to repeat itself in an infinite loop. No changes can be made; all choices are exact to the syllable. Every reaction is measured and practiced an infinite number of times. It is the greatest weight, says Nietzsche. If every choice, every action, is to be repeated an infinite number of times, my next choice would determine my fate for infinity to come, as would the choice after that. If I can't look back and say I would do it all again, down to every last breath, then I would be directly denying life or wishing for a life that was not and could never be, also a denial of life. Life is as is or not at all. No do overs. No buts. I had to live in a way that made me gracious for life every day, but which way was that?

I might have become a man, but I had no idea what I was going to do about it.

The automatic Wal-Mart doors parted, and I was reborn into the morning light. The smell of hot asphalt wafted through my nose, and the noise of car engines filled the air on the walk to my van in the back of the lot. Everything had changed, but nothing was different. I pulled myself behind the steering wheel and into the familiar seat for the first time.

Part II

A New Man

9. Adam in the Garden of Eden

Sequoias are the largest trees on Earth by volume. I had seen them before, but my memory of the giants was unclear at best.

I still felt a little sick from L.A., but once skyscrapers and grey buildings turned into big trees, green forests, and blue lakes, I felt better.

I drove through the first part of the park until I found a couple buildings and a parking spot where I could sleep for the night because campgrounds were full. I did a short, nearby hike and spent the rest of the evening at a secluded picnic area to watch the sunset over a canyon.

After breakfast I drove to the main part of the park. Near the visitor's center, tourists were thick, so I drove further until the population thinned out.

I parked at the trailhead that went past General Sherman: the largest tree in the world. What an incredible view it was to see something so massive and know that it was living. Looking at the tree gives an excellent perspective of human size. Our problems are small, finite, and short-lived. We are insignificant. Though we are alive and have built big, great things, nothing we could ever build could surpass the beauty of the world around us.

The hike led back to the visitor's center, past waterfalls and through the forest. I wandered through the visitor's center and learned a lot more facts about the area's history, trees, forest fires, lakes, and the life that was tied to the forest.

Worn out and ready for dinner, I returned to my van on the same trail.

I kept driving until I came to a campground on the border of Sequoia and King's Canyon National Parks where I reserved a site and immediately got a fire going. I was becoming much more comfortable with the van life and accustomed to a simple life. I had a quick meal heated by the flames.

When golden hour hit, I wandered around the site to take photos. I tried to capture smoke from campfires rising through the trees and being pierced by sun beams. When I looked at the photos, though, the smoke is not what I captured. My lens was in line with a sun beam, and it created a perfect circle of light on the photo. It looked cool, and I tried to capture the same thing but better and with purpose this time. I ended up with one of the best, most natural and creative images I had taken up to that point and was thrilled with how far I was coming in the work of photography.

In the morning, I drove north several hours through miles of construction, hours towards a different national park.

After a gate, the road led through a tunnel, which turned into bumper-to-bumper traffic. Like the car in front of me, I pulled off at the first opportunity. Before me sprawled the picturesque Yosemite Valley. Half Dome stood out on the far side, and between us were gushing waterfalls, heavy with spring snowmelt. The valley was a lush green, the cliff faces gray granite, waterfalls white, and sky baby blue. Wisps of clouds hung lazily in the sky, not sure if they wanted to disappear into the ether or to stick around a while longer to take in more of the majesty below them. The road wound down into the valley at a pace equivalent to a crawl. I did not mind, though, because it gave me plenty of time to look out the windows and take in the majesty of Yosemite.

The main road in the valley was a long loop through the valley, circling back to the main road I came in on. I went around twice, trying to either find a place to park or a campsite. The park was bursting with tourists, so my chances of getting a site were slim to none. Still, I stopped at the park office. I was given the last, the very last open spot, and only for the one night. All the sites were fully booked out months in advance.

I was assigned to North Pines Campground at a site on the riverbank. After I parked, I stayed only long enough to add a few snacks and water to my backpack.

I walked down the road, following the signs to Mirror Lake. I had no plans or goals for my time in Yosemite other than to hike something big and see as much as I could. It was too late in the day for a long, steep hike, and Mirror Lake required little effort to reach. It was the closest destination to my site. True to its name, Mirror Lake perfectly reflected the trees skirting the lake, the sharp granite cliffs that towered over the trees, and the brilliant blue of the cloudless heavens.

The next stop was Yosemite Falls, one of the most picturesque places in the park. The park had calmed down immensely, and I found a parking spot at the base of the falls. The dirt trail with its wooden bridges passed through thick brush and spiderweb streams emanating from the bottom pool of the massive waterfall. At Lower Falls, the roar was deafening, and the spray was intoxicating. The roar of the falls was like a constant roll of thunder over the Midwest plains.

The trail intersected with a few other paths, and I moseyed down a couple of them after leaving the bottom of the falls. Various points along the walk offered views up at the iconic waterfall. I wandered back to the parking lot and took a few snapshots of the surrounding views, one of which had a definite Ansel Adams vibe, which excited me. I was growing as a photographer and was learning how to capture certain effects on purpose. I was starting to develop a style.

Dusk fell, and I returned to my campsite for a warm can of soup and a small fire. A memory came back to me as I tried to drift off to sleep. I had been to Yosemite before as a small child with my family, and though I could remember few details, I remember going to a ranger talk in the evening, right at the base of one of the cliffs, and being told the legend of the wolverine by one of the rangers.

I called my best friends that night and learned they were planning to visit me in a few weeks when I got to Seattle. They were going to hang with me for a few days and wanted to do some hikes and go to a concert somewhere in the Seattle area. A paint rave we all wanted to go to was happening the weekend they would be there, so we bought tickets. I was thrilled they were coming to see me. When you leave home, most people ask when you're coming back. Only your real friends ask when they can visit you.

In the morning, I stopped by the ranger office to see if any cancellations had opened up another campsite. By the time I got there, I was already number 50 in line, so I knew it would be impossible to stay in the valley another night.

I drove back to Yosemite Falls and found the trailhead to Yosemite Point. The trail switch-backed its way up the granite cliffs and behind the falls before going up to the edge of a cliff and crossing the stream that was about to fall thousands of feet to the valley below. The trail was moderately busy until about halfway up, at the point where a hiker could see the bottom of Upper Falls and the top of Lower Falls. After that, most of the people turned around, and the more prepared hikers continued to the top.

It was about here where I met Leo, a German man about my age who had been backpacking across the western part of the U.S. by himself for the last month.

We had the same pace and talked a lot on the way up about our travels and where we had come from. At one point he hesitated about turning back. He was staying in a hostel an hour and a half down the road, and the last shuttle there was leaving Yosemite soon. He thought he could make it if he ran down the trail. I told him I'd give him a ride since I was going that way anyway. I hoped I could stay at the hostel, too. I needed a shower.

After crossing the bridge on top of Yosemite falls, we got a little lost and ended up wandering to an overlook above Yosemite point with an even better view of the valley and surrounding mountains. There, we sat down and ate our lunches.

We took photos from the top and started to make our way back down. About halfway down, we came across a Brazilian girl who Leo recognized from the hostel. She was planning on hitchhiking her way back to the hostel, but I told her she could just hop in with Leo and me if she wanted. At the bottom, we piled into the van, and I drove us all to the hostel through granite canyons, next to and across white water rivers, up and down steep mountain roads until we were into the forest that surrounds Yosemite.

We found the hostel after a couple wrong turns. Unfortunately, it was totally booked, and the manager would not let me sleep in my van in the parking lot and use the bathrooms even if I paid for the night. I said goodbye to my new friends after adding them on Facebook and went down the road until I found a nice pull-off near a river where I could sleep. I was exhausted after the long day.

A few days before, while back in the Sequoias, I called Jason. Jason was Martin's brother, and I had never met him before. He lived in Santa Cruz, which was a very welcome detour before going into San Francisco. I would be meeting up with him the next night and maybe crashing at his place for the next couple days.

As I got closer to the ocean and Santa Cruz, I saw more and more shirtless people skateboarding down the street and people of all ages carrying surf boards. Per usual when driving into towns, I took a few wrong turns before finding Jason's house.

I had no idea what to expect when I knocked on his door, but I was greeted with a friendly smile from a jolly looking man. Jason had not been involved with my part of the Bergland side of the family for most of his life, and he was excited about the opportunity to meet more of his family and hear about how everyone he hadn't heard from in decades was doing.

We gathered up chairs and a parasol and then walked down to the beach to catch up and talk about the family and old memories while watching the surf and watching for dolphins.

The next day and a half was spent getting to know Jason. For the time I spent there, he had an open schedule, so he was able to take time to show me around. He helped me with computer stuff and gave me a ton of music. He had a few guitars, so we had a little jam session, and then we went to the pier to a restaurant where we watched sea lions swim and splash around in the ocean.

My last full day in town was all about exploring Santa Cruz. We went around town, drove up and down the coast, and went to the surf museum. For a late lunch we went to the wharf and ate at a place that cooked fresh catches from the day. I had a swordfish steak and a small bowl of clam chowder. It was incredible. It was some of the freshest fish I had ever had, and the clam chowder was something to include in a memoir.

In the evening we went to Best Buy, and Jason bought me an external hard drive when he learned I was photographer and didn't have a place to back up my photos. He helped me clone my hard drive since I had no idea what I was doing. I was thrilled to meet him. He seemed like a good person, like the rest of our family. I hoped he would start to do more with the rest of us who he felt estranged from.

After saying goodbye to Jason, I turned out of his neighborhood and got back onto Highway 1 to San Francisco. An hour away from the city, fog settled on the road, telling me I was getting close.

My dad's college roommate and his husband had recently bought a home in San Francisco, and that is where I was headed. They had offered to put me up for a few days and to employ me as a landscaper for some of their garden and landscaping projects.

I found their house without much of a problem, but finding a parking spot and maneuvering through the narrow streets turned out to be much more of a challenge than I thought it would be. It took a few laps around the block until I found somewhere to park.

One of their friends was visiting and joining us for dinner. I had told them I would be arriving around dinner time, so they all waited for me to get there before we went to a nice Italian restaurant down the street and had wine and an amazing charcuterie board.

Upon our return to the house, they set me up with a bed in the guest room with my own bathroom. It almost felt wrong to have a private bathroom. I had gotten used to running to public restrooms or digging a hole whenever I had to poop.

The next day I wanted to walk. It had been a few days since I had been on a long hike, so I left the house early and walked downtown. I explored a chunk of the bigger buildings of San Francisco and walked about fifteen miles before getting an Uber to take me back. That was my first time taking an Uber, so it was kind of exciting.

Collin and Steve were both home when I got back, and they told me about the work they needed done. They needed some landscaping work, their garden cleaned up, a few plants trimmed, and a few plants planted. They would pay me half of the going rate for a good landscaper in the area. I gratefully accepted; the going rate was generous. The whole next day I worked in their garden and made some much-needed money. I had already gone through almost half the money I started with.

Before getting to San Francisco, Collin and Steve asked if I wanted to go to a gala for the symphony orchestra Steve played in. It sounded fun but also like something I would have to dress up for, and I wasn't travelling with any nice clothes or dress shoes. I only had khakis and one button up shirt. But I also didn't really care much about my appearance and thought it would probably be more fun if I was underdressed, so I accepted. They told me not to worry about dress shoes or anything like that. When it came time to go to the gala, they gave me a pair of dress shoes, and I shaved my face. It surprised me a little that I could still clean up well, and it felt weird to wear something other than hiking boots.

The gala was held in a nice banquet hall in a beautiful building downtown. Everyone was dressed to the nines. The food was great. Beer and wine were free. Everyone I sat near was a doctor or held some prestigious position. After dinner was an auction fundraiser for the symphony orchestra, and people were donating thousands of dollars like it was nothing. It was all extravagant.

The weirdest part about it was that I didn't feel out of place. I had been to several banquets and fancy events for various purposes while growing up. Overall, I had enjoyed those sorts of things. After being a bum for even a couple months, I saw the silliness of it all. I had never taken ritual or extravagance too seriously, but I knew that, as an entrepreneur, I would be exposed to a lot of it. I could feel a split, or some sort of duality show itself in me about which type of life I wanted to lead. Could I maintain a foothold in both worlds, or would I have to choose one? How much of a contradiction would it be to be a successful entrepreneurial dirtbag? And what does success really mean? At the end of the day, I just wanted to be happy.

I spent most of the next morning working in the backyard finishing up the landscaping projects. I cleaned up a lot and planted some flowers and a lime tree. Digging the three-foot-deep hole and getting the heavy, dirt-laden tree out of the massive ceramic pot by myself was a bit of a challenge, but it ended up working out. Most summers of my life, my mom planted and tended multiple fruit, vegetable, herb, and flower gardens at home in our four-acre yard. Naturally, my brother and I ended up helping out a lot over the years, so I grew up to appreciate and enjoy working in the dirt. If anything, I was a little disappointed there was nothing more to do in their little backyard.

I finished around noon and then drove to the Golden Gate Park to explore while I waited to meet up with Emilie, a girl I had matched with on Tinder the night before. I went on a long walk around some of the ponds, took some photos of ducks, then walked to the Japanese tea garden. A few minutes before they closed, I ordered some tea and drank it while walking around that portion of the beautiful park. Many plants, bridges and statues filled the peaceful, overcast garden.

I met Emilie in a record store a few blocks away from the park. She was a promoter for a record label, so she was there to hang up some posters and wanted to peruse some records for her collection.

She showed me around downtown and told me about some cool local stuff. Apparently, during one of the seasons, there's this thing called the two o'clock titty. At two in the afternoon, a shadow of St. Mary's Cathedral falls on one of the massive grey buildings, and the shadow looks like side-boob. We walked halfway out onto the Golden Gate Bridge and talked about Alcatraz and about how the bridge was an infamous place for people to go to kill themselves by jumping into the harbor. Then on a lighter note, we went to Ghirardelli square, where we got chocolate covered strawberries and sat and chatted for a while. Emilie had to leave for work earlier than expected, so I had her drop me off in Chinatown. My van was still several miles away at the record store, but I welcomed the walk.

I wandered up and down the length of Chinatown and explored a few side streets and shops along the way. Everything was bright and colorful, and the restaurants made most of Chinatown smell really good. That night, the plan was for me to make sushi for Steve and Collin, so in one of the stores, I picked up a few sets of chopsticks and a bamboo rolling mat. It was a long walk back to my van, but I enjoyed it. I'm not much of a city person, but I can appreciate the beauty of cities and architecture so long as I don't spend too much time in a concrete jungle.

That night was my last night with Collin and Steve in San Francisco. With their help, a massive plate was quickly filled with sushi. We sat down to eat. Steve and my dad went to college together and were roommates for four years, so I got to hear some fun stories about a much younger version of my dad. He wasn't a party animal, but it was good to learn that my dad wasn't a goody-two-shoes! After dinner, Steve made a couple old fashioned cocktails before saying our goodbyes. We would miss each other the next morning because they were leaving for work early, and I was planning on sleeping in.

When I finally got up, I ate breakfast late, read for a while, and then hit the road in the afternoon.

I looked ahead for a place to sleep while waiting in traffic to leave the city. I did not want to make the trek to the Redwoods from San Francisco in one leap. A small town called Nice was about halfway between the two points, and though it was out of the way, the small town was on the shore of a lake and at the Southern edge of a national forest. I thought it could be a nice place to stay. The pun was the deciding factor, and after exiting Highway 101, I wound my way through the mountains to find Nice.

Right on the lake and before entering the town, I found a small park with a few short trails going into the trees. A couple of people sat on a bench in the open, green space that stretched from the small parking lot to the tree line. They seemed harmless enough, laughing and passing a blunt back and forth. I figured at least one of them was homeless.

The man was peculiar. He had long, grey hair, a scruffy grey beard, a heavy bull ring in his nose, a dirty tie-dye shirt, and tattered jeans. He looked like a homeless, gay ex-biker, and from his body language, I could tell he was not going to move from that bench any time soon, even after his friend left.

I had recently washed my clothes but had not yet folded them, so while he stared at the van, I folded clothes and vacuumed a little bit. I glanced out the windshield to find the man was still sitting on the bench, taking curious and long glances at the van.

The day was perfect: 70 degrees and sunny. It was evening, and I wanted to get out and walk around. I knew if I left the van, the chances of getting caught up in a conversation with the guy on the bench was high, and considering the looks I had been getting, I wanted to avoid that if possible. I had kept myself busy for almost three hours, and a few people had come and gone to the park and talked with the man.

I got tired of sitting in the van. I sized up the man on the bench. He was shorter than I was, but a little stockier, and by my guess, he was around 45 years old. After watching his facial expressions while talking to his friends who visited him, coupled with his attire, my initial feeling that he was relatively harmless was holding true. I think at this point, I also wanted to see how close I could get myself to potential danger and get out of it. I had gotten used to being around wild animals and finding myself in the occasional sketchy situation on a mountain or in a forest, but so far, all my interactions with people had been nothing short of pleasant. I had also gotten good at reading people, and I had been thinking I would be able to talk myself out of almost any situation and to avoid physical confrontation.

No one knew where I was other than north of San Francisco. It could be dangerous, and that only fueled my desire to get out of the van. It was all a gamble, and I felt like placing a bet. Just to be safe, I put a knife on my belt that was covered by my shirt. I wore a backpack that contained a jug of water and bear mace. I got out of the driver's seat and grabbed my walking stick out the back door. The only people in the area were the man on the bench and me. I could feel him looking at me from the second I opened the driver door.

The park was not big by any stretch of the imagination, so the short walk through the grass to the trails in the trees passed right by the occupied bench. Almost immediately, after I set foot on the grass, the man called out a greeting, and I responded in kind with a simple hello. He asked how my day was. I told him it was good so far, and he got up and walked over to me. My grip on the stick tightened slightly, and he smiled as he asked if I was from the area, already knowing the answer. I said no, and he asked if I wanted a tour of the park, if I wanted to know the history of it. I said sure, curious to see where this rabbit hole would lead.

From the time I stepped out of the van, a constant, small stream of adrenaline trickled through my veins. I followed him into the trees as he cheerfully told me some information about the town, when the park was established, the types of plants in the area. As he played the tour guide, he picked wildflowers and braided their stems absentmindedly. The first few minutes of this interaction was going well, but not surprisingly, the tone shifted a little after we had gone a fair distance down the trail, after it got narrower. He told me how he became homeless, how he was gay and had been on a streak of physically abusive boyfriends before being almost killed. He had decided to run away and be homeless. He talked about how he lived in the back of the park and was trying to convince the city to build him a shelter and allow him to be the groundskeeper.

94

I kept silent for the most part, going along with the conversation, asking, or answering a small question here and there. After he started talking about his tent home in the back of the park, I was more on guard, but displayed what I thought was a calm, chill, neutral demeanor. At a fork in the trail, one path went further into the woods to his tent, and the other looked like it would end back at the parking lot. Without breaking stride, I started walking down the latter.

He was almost done with weaving the stems of the small flowers together, and his conversation shifted again to his sexual exploits. I was doubly glad I went down the trail that led back to the parking lot, and slightly quickened my pace. The trees started opening up, and he slowed his pace. He asked again if I was from around the area. I said I was not. He asked if I knew anything about the area. I said I did not. He stopped walking, looked me dead in the eyes, and asked if I had been told the nickname of this park. My right hand went to my side and rested on the hilt of my knife through the shirt. I told him I had not.

Cocksucker Park! That was what the locals called it. He explained with a satisfied giggle that he was the cocksucker in residence. In the patch of trees just up the trail in sight of the parking lot was where he sucked most people's cocks. I started walking again, and he matched my pace. Did I want my cock sucked? He was good at it. I thanked him for the offer but turned him down; that's not how I rolled. He asked if I wanted to fuck him. I again said thanks, followed by a no. The sun was starting to set, and he asked what my plans were for the evening. I said I was going to drive into the national forest and find somewhere to camp. He asked if I wanted him to come with me and get my cock sucked. Again, I said no. He told me that he was good at sucking cock and how that was not coming from him, that is what everyone had told him.

At this point, my van was only a handful of strides away. I was trying to end the conversation, saying I needed to get going, but he was still following me. He stopped again and told me he would suck my cock. At this point, I knew he just wanted a little bit of validation and would try and try until he got it. I told him if I changed my mind and wanted my cock sucked, I would come back to the park and find him. That seemed to satisfy him, and he smiled. He wished me a fun journey into the national forest and said he looked forward to seeing me later.

I waved goodbye, got into the van, and drove the remaining four hours in the dark to the Humboldt County Redwoods. I pulled into a campsite around midnight and fell asleep, exhausted from the drive and the encounter.

In the morning I found a camp payment notice on my windshield from the camp host because I arrived too late to pay. On my way out of the camp the next morning, I stopped by the camp host, paid, and chatted for a while about the trees. She told me where I should go in each part of the Redwoods and gave me a map.

I was really wanting to get lost that day, just run into the forest, and run around like a child where no one could find me. The map showed a section of the interior part of the country park as state wilderness. No trails went that deep into the park, and there were a couple stream crossings. It sounded like heaven. I drove to the trailhead of the trail that would get me the closest to the interior.

After hiking a mile, I turned off the trail to head through the forest towards the wilderness. I found a section of the stream where a redwood had fallen. I climbed up it and walked all the way across the tree bridge. Then I walked probably an hour or two into the forest.

I came to a spot where I had to climb up a fallen tree like it was a boulder, and when I got to the top, I was awestruck. Before me laid out one of the most incredible views I had ever seen. This part of the forest was almost entirely untouched and not serviced, so it was truly wild.

Redwoods are the tallest trees on earth, the tallest being 380 feet. It is impossible to appreciate the entire beauty of these trees because from the ground, one cannot see the tops. Redwoods are impossibly wide things, too, over 20 feet in diameter. The ancient forest had a Jurassic atmosphere. I could feel the power and the wisdom of these impressive trees, both standing and fallen.

The giants dwarfed the large ferns and other plants on the forest floor. Even the trees that were the height of an average tree looked like small shrubs next to the giants. I felt utterly alone as I stood in awe looking out onto this incredible scene. My smile widened.

I unslung my backpack and took off my clothes. This place was exactly what I imagined the Garden of Eden must be like, and I did not want to soil it by being clothed. I did keep my boots on, though, because I couldn't see the ground in a lot of places. I did not need a broken stick through my foot. I waded through the sea of greenery, hands brushing through the ferns, committing their feel to memory.

Climbing a fallen tree naked was my next activity. On the top of the tree, the trunk was a walkway with an elevated view of the forest for a few hundred feet.

With crossed legs, I sat in the middle of the tree, still and quiet. If my presence had disturbed anything, I wanted it to become more comfortable with my being there. I wanted to see and hear the songs of the trees and ferns as if there was no such thing as a human. The voice started with a whisper. The forest came alive and started talking to itself and ignoring me. I felt so connected to it all.

On the forest floor after climbing down, I wandered again through the ferns until I found a stump where I could sit to eat. I had a few granola bars and an apple. I sipped my water from my two-liter bag. Roaming took up about another hour of my time before I started to head in the general direction of my van.

The downside of not wearing pants became painfully clear to me on my walk. I walked around a fern, and a jagged stick poking up from the ground cut my leg just above the knee. Although not too deep, it still bled some and dripped down my leg. I dabbed the blood with leaves and stuck a leaf to the cut with some spit. I let it sit for a little while until it dried. I had a first aid kit with me. I always did. I just did not want to use it.

Clothed again, I used a compass and the park map to make it back to the stream I had crossed, and from there, I found my way to the van. I left the northern part of the county park as the sun was starting to set and drove further north to Eureka.

I saw a shopping center where I figured I would sleep before spending the next few days in the state and national parks. Not long before twilight, I pulled into a parking lot off the side of the shopping center near some parked trailers.

I had just finished another cold soup dinner when I heard a knock at my window. I pulled the curtain aside. A tweaker with a lot of sloppily done face tats, a few piercings, long greasy black hair, a shoulder pack, and a ripped shirt asked if I was about to get out of town. I said I would in the morning, and he asked if he could come with me. I said no. He said please. I told him no, sorry, and stared hard at him while he thought about asking again.

After I watched him walk out of the parking lot, I drove around the small town to look for somewhere else to sleep. Nowhere else looked much better, so I went back to the shopping center's main lot even though I saw posted signs that forbade sleeping in vehicles.

Knocking woke me up late in the night, along with a light. The security guard stood waiting at my front window. He told me I could not stay. I needed to get out. Sleepily, I rolled the van across the side street to the back of a McDonalds parking lot and passed out. Not much later, another knock woke me up again. The same guard told me he was sorry, but I needed to move again. I could not stay in the McDonalds lot either. I was too sleepy to drive anywhere safely, so I explained that I was on a road trip and just passing through. I was tired and needed to sleep and would leave in the morning.

He wrestled with that for a second and then gave in. His voice softened from the gruff tone he used the first time I answered his knock. He told me the adjacent street was where they sometimes let truckers sleep, and that if I parked there and promised to be gone before 8 a.m., he would not bother me again. I thanked him, relocated, and dropped like a rock into bed.

At 7:30, I made a beeline for the next town up the road, Arcadia, which was significantly nicer than Eureka. Not nice in the sense of bigger, fancier houses, but the air of the town was more hippieish and friendly.

I found a coffee shop and got a hot latte to shake the remaining sleep from my brain. I parked near the ocean and laid in bed for a little while. I wanted a lazy day before going into the Redwood National and State Parks. I mostly read and swiped on Tinder. I matched with this girl, Rose, and neither of us had any real plans that day. So, we decided to meet up at a café a few hours later.

Rose and I chatted over coffee for a little while and talked about things to do and see in the towns around the Redwood parks and good spots of coastline. One of these beautiful coastal shorelines was in Trinidad, just up the road a few dozen miles. I followed behind her up the road until she turned off and followed a narrow, winding road to a gravel pull-off on top of a cliff. A trail started there and stretched out to another cliff farther out into the sea. We sat out there for a while and told each other stories. Then she wanted to go somewhere else.

In a nearby town was a beach where a lot of people surfed. It was also a popular spot for college kids to come and drink, hence the name College Beach. We made our way down the beach and climbed up a rock spire that jutted up from the black sand. She showed me some of her tattoos, and I talked about the tattoos I wanted. The conversation led to us making out on top of the spire in the middle of a bright blue day, salty waves crashing in the background.

She had to work in the evening, so we split up. She went back south to Arcadia, and I went north to the Redwoods, hopefully to meet up later.

I found a good campground on the southern outskirt of the parks, with wild moose grazing on the grassy area at the side of the road. I paid for a few nights and a couple bundles of firewood. I found my spot, got the wood set up for a fire later in the evening, then drove north.

The side of the road became the sea, and I parked to watch the sunset. The sun lowered itself from the clear sky into the sea. When the sun had drowned and the colors that danced on the water became grey, I returned to the campground and lit my fire. I did not see Rose that night, or again.

The next day I went to the middle of the park and hiked as many trails as I could. I pulled off onto most pull-offs in the park. The morning fog did not dissipate until the afternoon, which made the forest moody, mysterious, and quiet.

One of the roads I went down to was the road to Fern Canyon. The road was dirt and wound through the forest like a lost snake. I probably should not have taken my van down that road; there were a few extremely tight turns I barely made, but that just made it more of an adventure.

I arrived at the entrance to Fern Canyon, but the ranger who was supposed to be at the gate was gone. The arm blocking the road was down. I did not see any signs on how I was supposed to enter, and there was nowhere to park on that side of the gate. So, I turned around and drove the 25 minutes back through the heavy, wet air darkened by the thick canopy overhead.

In the Redwoods, I mostly did day hikes. I should have done more distance hikes and spent nights alone under the immense trees, but for some reason I just was not in the mood for it. I had the energy but lacked the desire. One of the shorter trails I hiked, probably my favorite short hike in the Redwoods, was in Ladybird Johnson Grove. The trail was wide and easy. It felt like I was walking through time. The forest felt ancient, proud, and wise.

For two days I wandered around different parts of the forest, seeing the tallest trees and a few deer here and there. I spent a lot of quiet time reflecting about how I ended up here and what my life was turning into. So far, this trip had been the most difficult thing I had ever done in my life, but so many amazing things happened to me to that I would have never otherwise experienced. Looking forward, I felt that trend would continue. As I became more comfortable navigating the world, I would be able to get into even crazier and more amazing experiences.

On the flip side, things were also going to get much more difficult. My bank account had been buffed up enough from the work I had done in California that I was more confident I could make it through Canada with the money I had. The exchange rate helped, too. My calculations focused on gas and oil changes. After Canada, I didn't know what I was going to do.

My food budget was next to nothing, I was already eating less than I should, and I was burning more calories than I was consuming. The math was not hard, and I knew it was only a matter of time before I would know hunger like I had never known before. My diet up to this point primarily consisted of a roll or two in the morning, a can of soup for lunch if I was not hiking, a sandwich if I was, or a few handfuls of trail mix if I was driving. For dinner, I would eat either a can of soup or a handful of trail mix. Even that approximately four-dollars-a-day-diet was going to be compromised going forward.

Meditating in the forest helped clear my mind and got me ready for the next border I was about to hop. On the way back to the campground, I stopped by the ocean to see the sunset, but the cloudy, grey sky hardly changed color at all before the day began to grow dark. I got to the campground and woke up a few sleeping moose in the grassy areas of my site. I quickly got a fire going and put a can of chunky soup on the grate above the flames. The night was chilly.

A few sites over from me that night was a group of friends who came out there to drink in the woods, see the magnificent trees, and get away from everyday life for a little while. I had a fire of my own and sipped my beer through the night. Seeing and hearing the group laugh and joke around their fire and in the woods sent a pang of loneliness through me, but not as unbearable a feeling as I experienced closer to the beginning of the trip.

In the weeks before I left, I texted a lot of my friends in St. Joe and tried to hang out with as many people as I could before I went off on my own. Most of the people I reached out to never even responded. Most of those who did were too busy, save for a very close few.

I wouldn't say I was popular in high school. I knew the cool kids, but we never hung out or partied. I wasn't on the fringes or in the background either. I was in that weird in-between place. I did not have problems with anyone, and I was involved with various activities around the school from band to sports to business and art clubs. I never had a group of friends, though. I was not in any group chats. I did not play video games, which is how a lot of friend groups interacted out of school. I tried to stay busy and productive as much as I could after school, limiting my time and desire to hang out with school friends.

Most acquaintances were quick to slip away when graduation passed. Most of my friends had gone off for university, but I stayed at home. Most people from high school who remained in the area were doing their own thing, and I did mine. I was working on my dreams and goals.

My driven, dreaming mindset was another barrier to connecting with people at home. The separation from the general norm of my generation was one of the things that motivated me to do something for myself and to surround myself with people who had similar energy and passion for their dreams.

Seeing the group of friends in the forest was the first time I sat around and analyzed my own friendships. I was endlessly glad to have left home and high school behind. I was sad but kind of relieved to realize that most of my friends had started to become and would continue to transition back into strangers who I might catch up with at high school reunions every decade or two. But that was okay. I had already met many new, fascinating people. I had become close with strangers in the span of a couple days. I knew my life would be full of friendship and love wherever I was.

The morning brought fog, asphalt, and painted lines dividing the road. All signs and arrows pointed north to Oregon. I followed.

10. Up and Down the Mountain

In Oregon, I wanted to visit Megan in Eugene for a few days, and I wanted to see Crater Lake.

Megan and I met on Tinder when I was in Zion, and we had been talking via text for more than a month. I liked her. She was smart, outdoorsy, funny, and listened to me when I needed to talk to someone. She was a cool girl, and we definitely had a connection. I still hadn't fully gotten over my last girlfriend. It seems first love tends to stick around forever, but Megan was starting to make me forget about her for a little bit.

I was nervous. I hadn't seen her in person yet, but I could tell I was going to like her. She had dogs, grew up on a farm, and wasn't afraid to get dirty. I was nervous because I knew I would like her, but I wouldn't be able to stay there with her. It would be a long time before I could come back, if ever.

I also wanted to spend time on the coast. The Oregon coastline is all state-owned public land, so it is kept natural and beautiful. I had plenty of time to kill before meeting up with Megan and no real direction, so I drove slowly and took in as much of the scenery as I could.

I reached Medford in the afternoon and drove around the town. I think Medford would be a nice place to live. It is a sizeable town with the amenities and comforts one could want, and the surrounding nature is beautiful. It is not too far from the coast, either. Most of the buildings were not more than a few stories. The town felt homey and tucked away.

I have never been an anxious or nervous person, but something was gnawing at me. I was parked in the back of a shopping center lot trying to make myself a sandwich, and my foot would not stop tapping. My whole right leg was shaking. My heart felt like it was going to jump out of my chest so I could watch it beat on the bed beside me, convulsing as a troubled heart does. I could not eat. I had not eaten all day, but I could not choke down a single bite of my sandwich. My stomach refused to accept anything save the smallest sips of water. It had gotten dark and chilly, so I put on a hoodie and lay down, hoping to relax. Maybe if I could close my eyes, my heart would stop trying to tear itself out of my throat. It felt like forever, but the anxiety attack probably lasted only 20 minutes.

Even though the worst of it was over, I still could not sleep. My mind picked up where my heart and leg left off as it began racing. I was worried about meeting Megan and what would happen after I left. I would be in new territory and then into a new country on my own. I was excited because the Pacific Northwest was the region I looked forward to most, but it was also the area I knew the least about.

It was late, but I was still wide awake. I crawled out of bed and left my pillow wetted with anxious tears and put on pajama pants and a sweater. I took a couple bites of the sandwich that was still sitting on my cooler and climbed into the captain's chair. The sound of the engine starting revved my heart, and the anxiety crawled back. I blasted music over the radio. I needed to move. I needed to move. I needed to move.

I threw the van into drive and sped out of the parking lot back onto the dark road. I did not care where I went. I just drove north.

Barreling down the highway, I came to the turn-off for Crater Lake. I took it and sped up the mountain. Buildings and asphalt were replaced with thick trees and winding dirt roads. The route took me by Lost Creek Lake which was occasionally lit by the pale moon intermittently poking through the twilight cloud cover. Everything around me seemed peaceful and quiet, but I felt like a tornado.

The road got steeper, and whispers of snowflakes in the air melted when they touched the cold glass of my windshield. I had the AC on and windows down. I was trying to freeze the panic in my bones since the warmth of blankets didn't seem to work. My foot was glued to the gas pedal, and I climbed the mountain faster. Snow was piled on the side of the road. Every ten minutes, the piles seemed to grow by five feet. The higher I went, the heavier the snow fell.

I passed through the gate to the park, and the grade increased again. So did the snowbanks. They must have been twenty feet tall. The road got steeper, and my foot pressed harder on the gas. The engine was alive and ready to reach the summit despite the snow-covered roads and poor visibility. I had nowhere else to go.

At the summit, I could see nothing but white. The snow on the shoulders could not have been less than twenty-five feet tall, and snow was building on the road. I parked on a small pull-off carved out of the snow and turned off my headlights. I gripped the wheel with white knuckles laid my forehead on the cool rubber cover, and counted my breaths. Eventually, the buzzing in my ears stopped.

Snow fluttered through the open window and gave me cool kisses on the back of my exposed neck. Deep breaths. Why had I driven all the way up to the summit? I had known exactly what I would find. I would find snowbanks and no visibility. I knew that from the first snowflake I saw falling through the night sky. My foot was still locked, pressing down hard, but it was off the pedal now. I'd go back down. There wasn't anything for me at the top of the mountain, and I didn't want to get stuck in the snow.

The drive down was slower. I exited the park gates, drove past the lake and to the same parking lot I had left earlier that night.

I turned off the van and sat on the end of my bed with my head in my hands. What the hell was I doing? Tonight, tomorrow, yesterday? What the hell was I doing? I had no plans, and it didn't feel like I had a direction at all. For this trip or beyond.

I wouldn't be sleeping that night. That much I knew. It was midnight, and the sun would rise in a few hours.

My leg started bouncing again, and I got behind the wheel, driving in silence with the windows down this time. At one point I screamed. I screamed as loud as I could until my voice was hoarse, and my throat was raw.

By the time I reached the summit of Crater Lake the second time, the snow was deeper.

I turned around again.

This time I stopped in a wide pull-off for overnight parking maybe ten miles from the Lake. I shut the van off, put boots on, and stood outside in the quiet snowfall. I tried to look for something in the forest on the side of the road. The whole night I had only seen two cars on the road. It was a quiet, cold night. My peacoat was dusted with a layer of snow when I climbed behind the wheel out of the cold.

I drove to the top of the mountain for a third time. I wished more than anything that I had someone in the passenger seat who would listen to me. I didn't even know what I would say, but I wanted to talk. I wanted to be heard. I had already spent so much time alone. I rarely hugged. I rarely shook hands. I was good at befriending people, but it didn't feel like I had any friends. There was no one I could just talk to for hours. The friends I made, I left. My brother had visited, and I had seen family and friends. Because I was changing and my surroundings were new to me, even the people I knew felt unfamiliar. I craved human connection. I just wanted to be hugged. To be held. To feel someone's lips on mine. I had spent too many nights alone in a cold bed in an uninsulated box.

I told myself I would continue down the road and keep going north this time, but now my foot wouldn't touch the gas pedal. I was tired, and my eyes started to droop.

I turned around again and parked in the pull-off by the trees. I killed the van and laid in bed on top of the blankets and stared at the ceiling until the first tendrils of light poked through the forest and lit up the dust particles floating in the van's air.

Coffee on the stove out of the back door, and a granola bar were breakfast.

Another drive through the gate took me up to the summit. Crater Lake is normally a caldera a few miles wide filled with the bluest water I have ever seen. It is a couple thousand feet from the rim of the blown-out volcano to the water. On the east side of the lake, there's an island dubbed Wizard Island since it looks like a wizard's hat. I could see none of that. It was still snowing, but I saw people this time. The shoulders of the road were filled with cars of people who would not get to see the lake through the mountains of powdery snow. Some people were climbing the massive snowbanks and playing in the snow.

After the painfully exhausting night, I needed something to lift my spirits. I needed something innocent and light after feeling broken. I bundled up, laced my boots tightly, and climbed to the top of a snowbank.

When I reached the top, I saw even taller drifts, so I kept going until I was at the very top. I leapt down and was instantly buried in the soft snow, and I made snow angels beneath the snow. For about an hour I just played and smiled and laughed in the soft snow. I felt a lot better in the day; that was the way it usually worked. Nights could be hard, but during the day, I could keep myself busy and happy.

My last trip to Crater Lake was the best of the four, but I did not feel like I could stick around much longer, I needed to leave the night behind me, and the best way to do that was to physically leave. I followed the road part of the way around the lake until it dropped from the summit and back into the forest. It was a beautiful drive, and I took it slow.

I drove out of the national park. I got on Hwy 138 through the forest until it met back up with I-5. That drive was one of the prettiest drives up to this point. Clouds hung low. Rivers were swift and clear. And wilderness was all around. With my windows down, I could almost feel the forest breathe. The tree-covered hills stretched up into the clouds and disappeared from view. I pulled off the road and sat to watch the clouds move sneakily through the hills.

After a while, I pulled back onto the road and continued down it. I didn't drive very far. Down the road a few miles was a wider pull-off right by a river. I parked facing the river with the road behind me. I unbuckled, put my socked feet on the dash, and watched the ice blue river slowly blur as fog covered the windshield. When I couldn't see the white of the rushing river anymore, I put on my rain jacket and went out the side door to sit on the bank. The air was sweet and heavy, and the river carried my worries downstream. I stayed there through the night. The night was cool, and I could hear the river softly through the thin metal walls of the van. When sleep finally came, it was not restful. I did not dream that night.

The next day I was going to meet Megan, and I was still nervous. I woke up late and ate a granola bar while river water heated up to a boil in the pot on my stove. I was chilly standing in the morning fog waiting for the water to boil, but it was too beautiful of a morning to be inside.

With a scalding mug of coffee in my cup holder, I started the van and finished the forested drive to I-5 North. I reached the University of Oregon. I looped around campus twice to find Megan's dorm. She lived in a very pretty, old brick building. She was standing out front waiting for me with a huge smile on her face. She hugged me as soon as I opened the driver's door.

She excitedly led me up her to her room so I could drop off my small bag of toiletries. We kissed, then went to the store for groceries for the couple days I would be there. The groceries we got ended up being closer to snack food except for yams and ketchup. She had boasted on her dorm-style sweet-potato-making prowess.

We walked around campus and talked a fair amount before ending up back in her room for food and tea in the evening. The next day she had just a couple classes in the morning. She got up and left while I took my time to roll out of bed and get showered in the floor bathroom. Once clean, I made some tea and set up my computer to edit photos and write a blog post while I waited for Megan to get out of class.

It felt cool to be on a college campus, and I started to think about how my college experience would be once I got back to the Midwest and had to completely change my lifestyle again. I was sure I would make the adjustment fine, but the thought of being in the same place for four years didn't sit right, especially now that I had tasted pure freedom as a vagabond.

I spent several days with Megan. She took me around the town. We went on hikes and walks in the area. We made love. She didn't have a roommate which made a lot of things easier. I don't think there would've been space for three people in her small dorm room.

Being with her was nice, but it was weird. Now that I was finally with Megan, it felt wrong. I waited a month to see her only to spend a couple days with her and never see her again. I liked her, and we had gotten to know each other well. But at the same time, it felt like a waste. It didn't feel like getting attached was fair to either me or her, but it was a little late for that thought because we had both started to catch feelings. We made the most of our time together, but the idea that this would be it for us loomed in the back of my mind. It was a poisonous thought.

I left on a weekend so we could sleep in on our last morning together. After breakfast, she helped me pack up the little I had brought and kissed me goodbye. I turned to get in the driver's seat, but she stopped me with, "Wait, before you go." She grabbed my arm. "I made these for you," she said. "Don't open the sheet with the song names until after you listen to the CD's all the way through." She smiled with her entire face.

I left Corvallis and Megan behind me and headed west to the coast. It was raining, and the road followed the tops of cliffs, offering the occasional overlook onto the sandy beaches and waves crashing below. The rain beat steadily, and the rhythm was hypnotizing. It was late afternoon, but there was still plenty of light left in the day.

I parked off the highway on an overlook. From the captain's chair I could see the beach and ocean a couple hundred feet below and a half mile out. The wind was gentle, and the air was chilly but not cold. In my hoodie and jeans, I crawled into the back half of my van and laid down. Looking at the patterned tapestry on the ceiling, I felt happier than I had in a while. I felt like everything was as it should be

I had come it a long way. I had gone through some hard things, both mentally and physically. I had seen life from different angles. I had met a girl. I was seeing the world. I was learning a lot. I was getting better at photography. I was not even halfway through my journey, and I was excited for what was to come.

I pulled Megan's gift out of my backpack and put the first disc into my laptop. I didn't have a CD player in the van. I put on a pair of headphones and hit play. I snagged a beer from under the bed, opened the bottle, took a swig, and laid back down.

I liked Megan's taste in music. The mix tapes were well organized. She put a lot of thought into making them. I didn't know most of the songs on the first two discs, but I liked them. The third CD was filled with classics, most of which I knew. It was hard to stop myself from opening the folded paper playlists, but I held off until the second-to-the-last song ended. The lists were labeled Road Tunes 1, 2, & 3, and they were all kick-ass road trip mix tapes. I put all the songs onto my iPod so I could listen to them through the van speakers while I was driving the next day.

By the time I finished listening to and transferring the songs, the sun had set behind the clouds, and darkness was creeping in. The rain continued softly beating on the metal roof. I fished out a can of beer and potato soup from under my bed and shook it before popping its tab. As it got darker, the cold increased. I put pajama pants on and crawled under the two comforters and two blankets. I drew the curtains closed, and the rain became my lullaby.

I woke up feeling better than I had ever felt after waking up. I don't know if it was the rain or the view I woke up to, but everything felt right. I felt like I could take on the world, and I was ready to get up and face anything. That was my first thought. My second was that I really had to shit. No toilets were at the overview. The closest town was ten miles away, and it was raining. I thought about trying the drive, but the second I moved my leg out from under the blankets, I knew I was in trouble.

I reached for my rain jacket, rain pants, and toilet paper. I didn't even tie my boots. I threw open the side door and sprinted across the empty parking spaces towards the patch of trees on the end of the parking lot and over the guard rail.

Fortunately, no one was on the road to see me try to run while clenching with my rain pants halfway on, my boots untied, and toilet paper trailing out of my hands. As soon as I passed the first tree on the other side of the guard rail, I pulled my pants down and sprayed the side of a tree. I cleaned up quickly and threw the dirty toilet paper away in the trash can by guard rail. I probably should have gone in a bucket. I got soaked and cold standing in the rain.

The side door of the van was still half open, and the inside van was getting wet. I went back inside, stripped out of my wet outer layer, and laid back down on top of the blankets. I wanted to make it to Washington that day, but I was in no rush

When I eventually got up, it was still morning, and the rain had let up. Rays of sun poked through the clouds and lit up patches of the ocean. I ate two several-day-old Danishes, chugged some water, and got into the driver's seat.

The coastline was beautiful, and the road followed as close as possible to the water. I stopped at a few of the beaches to sit on some rocks and look at the ocean. Around noon I stopped again to eat a sandwich on the beach and listen to the surf.

It was mid-afternoon by the time I made it up to Fort Stevens State Park. The state park is on the far Northwest end of Oregon. Mostly, the park is beach and trees on each side of the road. Megan told me I needed to go to the park to find the Wreck of the Peter Iredale and climb in it.

The wreck is little more than the rusty skeleton hull of a boat, but it is kind of fun to use as a jungle gym right on the beach. After the wreck and a couple stops at viewpoints, I made it to the very end of the road. I walked around the beach looking at Washington's coast across the ocean. I took some photos of the distant shoreline. I skipped some rocks across the ocean. None of them made it to the other side.

It started to rain again. Because I had my camera with me, I thought I should go back to the van. The wind picked up significantly on the walk back, and it almost blew me over. I drove back to the parking lot near the wreck because it was the closest lot with the best view of the beach. I pulled out a book and read for an hour or two and was again put into a trance by the soothing rain drops on the thin van roof.

Thinking about what I wanted to do in Washington, I knew I would have to go to a chiropractor. My neck had slipped out again, and I was changing.

Unless something quickly jars my neck out of place, my body slowly slips back to its injured state, changing me gradually. First, my short-term memory fades. I can set something down and lose it three seconds later. From short term memory lapses, I slip into a state of general forgetfulness. I might walk in a direction and forget where I'm going.

With increased brain fog comes a throbbing and dull, constant headache. I frustrate easily and have a much shorter temper. Then, as I struggle to form complex thought and ideas, I become reserved and quiet. I start to hide away from people. Sometimes I write.

Everything is opaque. During moments of clarity, I start to notice the changes in my personality. I see how it's harder to find the brighter side of things. I'm not nearly as creative. I lose interest in things I love to do. I'm selfish. In short, I become my opposite and the last type of person I want to be.

After my neck slips out, depending on how bad it is I may reach the point of self-realization anywhere from a week to two months later. Because of my stubbornness, I usually have to get to the point of noticing personality changes to seek help I need from a chiropractor. With one adjustment, I immediately feel the strangle hold around my spinal column loosen and my brain breathe again. The foggy veil lifts a little, and I continue to return to myself with each of the next few chiropractic visits.

If I don't get to a chiropractor when needed, the downward spiral quickens. When it gets bad, there is no "I" anymore; the I is lost. External stimuli are of little concern and hardly noticed. My body goes through the motions if it feels so compelled. Left alone, my body can sit for hours unmoving and unthinking. If a thought comes up, it is quickly swallowed and forgotten. I exist, but I am a shadow in constant agony. Existing in this way, in midnight fog, is not death. Nor is it life. It is temporal purgatory: a box made of two-way mirrors and no doors. I become invisible.

I don't want to go back to referring to my driver's license to remember who I am. I tremble at the thought what of might happen if the darkness of the fog becomes complete. I allow myself time to contemplate life, death, and suffering. I do not fear death. I have come close enough a few times in my life already, and I am comfortable enough with the idea of not existing anymore. Before I was born, I did not exist in the same way I won't exist after I die. Or maybe I always did exist and always will exist if soul is indeed eternal. Matter can neither be created nor destroyed, but what is soul? We are all small pieces of something much grander and much more beautiful than our senses or reason could never perceive. I do not think death should be feared; the inevitability of death is the last and most sure adventure for physical forms, so celebration is more appropriate than fear. Until that day comes, I want to make the most of my life and see all the wonders of the world. But to do that and to continue enjoying life while road tripping through it, I needed some help.

I spent the next hour talking with a friend in Seattle, asking for assistance finding a chiropractor in the area. So far from home, I needed to do something about my neck and do it quickly.

I left the park and got back on the 101 towards the border of Washington. The closest crossing over the Columbia River was through Astoria.
The bridge was a shadow in the darkening fog that became more pronounced as I got closer. I felt much like the bridge.

The rain sprinkled as I crossed the wide river.

11. Tomorrow May Never Happen Yesterday Will Never Happen Again

I drove until I saw a sign for a wildlife refuge. I pulled over at a picnic area off the road in the trees. Unlike the previous night, there was a small brick bathroom. I wouldn't have to dress up to find a tree in a rush the next morning. I was tired from the long day of driving, and sleep found me quickly my first night in Washington.

In the morning I skipped breakfast and went to the wildlife refuge. I spent a good part of the morning walking around on short trails, but I mostly walked bench to bench along the trails. I was not feeling too active. I wanted to take a day and chill. I had done a lot of hiking and being outdoors in the last couple months. I wanted a little break, while still being outdoors. I thought a lot about the trouble my best friends and I would get into when they flew into Seattle.

I lounged around in the van for another couple hours and then drove on. A couple hours past the wildlife refuge was Aberdeen, and I was done with driving by the time I got there. I explored the town a little bit and saw it had a large grocery store and several restaurants. I had rarely eaten out over the last few months. When I wasn't with family or friends, I might have only eaten out five times, mostly when I was feeling too lazy to cook or when it was cold and I wanted a warm meal. Restaurants were just too expensive, and there wasn't room in my budget.

After soul-warming freshly baked Pizza Hut pizza in Aberdeen, I went to the grocery store and parked in the back of the lot by some train tracks. I put pajamas on and opened the blinds to read. Next to the train tracks and the entrance to the parking lot, stood a man with a cardboard sign. He stood there for three hours. I felt bad for him. I felt like I had a much closer understanding of what he must be going through than I ever had before. I wanted to help, but I was in no financial situation to be able to help anyone. I had already finished the pizza. When the evening came and cars stopped coming in, he walked with his head down to a tan car in the back of the lot. It looked like he stuffed everything he owned into that tiny car. We both slept in that parking lot, and I felt like I had it easy.

I was eager for my drive when I woke up. I would make it to Olympic National Park that afternoon, one of the parks I looked forward to the most when starting the trip. Up the 101 from Aberdeen about an hour was Lake Quinault. I got up to the park and stopped for a walk around the lake. It was a little out of the way, but the pictures I Googled of it looked cool. So I went. When I got there, the clouds were so low over the lake I felt like I could jump up and touch them.

I got back on the road and soon saw a sign for a rainforest hostel. I hadn't seen many hostels in America, so I really wanted to know what this hostel looked like. The second sign I reached that said Rainforest Hostel pointed up a gravel driveway to a small, yellow house with a greenhouse beside it. Immediately next to the Rainforest Hostel sign was a Bernie Sanders poster with duct tape under the name and "DON'T GIVE UP!!" written on top of the tape. The 2016 presidential election was almost seven months ago. I sat parked on the shoulder for several minutes wondering if I should stay. I didn't need to stay at a hostel. I had no reason to since I had my van and there were plenty of places to park. But that hostel just looked like it would be an interesting experience.

I decided to think about it more. I kept driving up the road until I saw Ruby Beach. I parked in the almost-full lot and walked down the trail to the beautiful, black sand beach. A thick line of old driftwood trees pushed against the tree line after the trail popped out on the beach. A creek ran from the forest and fed into the ocean. I wandered around with my camera for an hour or so taking pictures. Near the water was a large rock with a hole through it. I took a few photos through the hole and then put my camera down. I considered it. The rock looked kind of familiar.

As I stared at the rock, a guy was walking down the beach not too far away. I asked if the rock looked like a vagina to him. He looked taken aback at first, then looked at the rock for a few seconds, and said it did kind of look like a vagina.

I decided to go back to the hostel and at least see the cost for a night. If it was cheap, I would stay. Besides, I could use a shower anyway. Mine was the only vehicle in the driveway when I pulled up, and the place was quiet. On the second set of knocks, the door was answered by an older man with white hair and suspenders that pulled his shoulders down. He just kind of looked at me for a little. He didn't say anything.

I asked if this was a hostel. He asked if I saw the Bernie sign out front. He peered at me a little longer and told me to follow him inside. I followed. A few feet into the house, I chuckled a little bit to myself. This guy was a nice old hippie who lived alone, had a lot of books, and tried to rely on the man as little as possible. I knew we were going to get along well.

He told me to sit on the couch, so I sat. For the next twenty minutes, he told me about how he still supported Bernie Sanders even though he lost. He believed in Bernie's ideals and believed that he was the best choice for America for a variety of reasons. Regardless of politics, the hostel owner wanted people to be able to politely disagree and have conversations about different views and perspectives. He thought Sanders would promote that tolerance. My host talked a while longer about politics and about how he was living with as small a footprint as possible. Then he asked me some questions about myself, what I was doing, and some of my political views.

He explained how he turned his house into a hostel to help travelers and to get to know people. Bed prices are based on what people can and want to pay. He suggests $10, but he asks his more financially stable guests to consider paying a little extra so people who aren't well-off can only pay a few dollars, evening costs out, with no one paying more than they think the night is worth. Regardless of how much people pay, they have to do twenty minutes of chores per night to help keep his house clean. He asked if I was still interested in staying.

I told him I still wanted to stay and gave him $15. He pulled out a local map from somewhere near him and started talking about beaches and other beautiful areas nearby. He loved this part of the Pacific Northwest. He told me to go to Ruby Beach first, then go into Olympic National Park. He told me a dozen other things about the area, too.

It was still kind of early in the afternoon, so I decided to go up to the closest entrance of the national park to get an idea of longer trails I wanted to do the next day. The entrance was within an hour, and the drive was through dense rainforest. Wet, green moss covered almost all the tree trunks in the woods I drove through. No rain was coming down, but the air was wet and heavy. It smelled like earth. Clouds clung to the tops of the trees and moved lazily through the sky.

On the road to the Hoh Rain Forest Visitor Center, I stopped at a small café and shop that mostly sold a bunch of Hoh River and Olympic National Park branded clothing, but the back corner had camping and outdoor gear. I ended up getting a backpacking stove, a one-liter aluminum pot, and propane. The propane and stove fit inside of the one-liter pot. I didn't use the Coleman stove I brought often because it required several minutes to set up and put away, and it was inefficient. In cold or wind, it might take 15 minutes to boil a pot of water. I had been looking at getting a new stove for the last month but just hadn't, and I felt good about supporting this little shop.

When I made it to the forest visitor center, the afternoon was still overcast. The PNW was the part of the trip I was most excited for, and I wanted to spend as much time outdoors here as possible. I hadn't done a solo overnight hike yet on this trip. I had a backpacking pack that was already packed to go, so I decided to give it a test run. If it felt good on a short hike, I would come back the next day and try a couple days on a longer trail that left from the same visitor's center.

The pack weighed maybe thirty pounds. The gear I brought wasn't made for backpacking, and I was very overpacked for one night in the woods. The pack lacked a waist strap and was chunky. Still, I threw it over my shoulders and started walking down the Hoh river trail. I was about a mile in when I had to take the pack off, rub my muscles, and readjust. Not having a waist strap killed my shoulders. I made another half mile before I had to take the pack off again. I went out to the bank of the river, took everything out of the pack, and repacked it so the weight was more evenly distributed. Repacking was a great excuse to sit on the bank of the river for a little while and watch the clean, blue water cut through the valley. This was exactly what I pictured Washington to be. It was beautiful beyond description. I felt so whole heartedly at peace sitting on that river, like that was where I needed to be.

I only made another mile down the trail before turning around. I couldn't hike with that pack. My shoulders and back were sore from the thin straps and awkward weight. If I ever went backpacking on this trip, I would have to get a new backpack, and that was probably not going to happen.

I got back to my van and unshouldered my pack. Pulling out a can of beer and potato soup, I used my new stove setup for the first time. The screw-on stove held the can perfectly and got the soup just short of boiling in only a minute or two. I sat at a picnic table in a clearing amidst trees and ate the warm soup. I was happy with my simple life. Sunset went unnoticed through the clouds, and the sky gently darkened as I finished the soup and packed up to go back to the hostel.

I saw another car when I pulled up to the small house. Four people were hanging out in the living room when I walked inside. I joined them, and we talked for a while about our trips and what we were wanting to do in the area. Of course, the host was quick to bring Bernie Sanders into the conversation. We talked for a couple hours, then went to bed. The others had a room with four beds to themselves, and I got a room with six bunk beds to myself. I cozied up in the thin, wool blankets and went right to sleep.

In the morning, we all got up about the same time. I came into the kitchen as the group was making eggs. They said they would throw in a couple more for me. I went out to my van and brought in some coffee to share. When the food was done and we sat down to eat, the host came in and set some hot sauce on the table, asking if any of us wanted it. He told us that it was homemade with peppers he grew. He suggested we try a small amount before putting it on our food, then walked back to the kitchen to get a plate. I have run into very few hot sauces I have not liked, so I thought he was talking about taste when he said to try it first. I did not try the sauce. Instead, I covered my eggs with it. When he came back into the room and saw my eggs, his eyes widened. He asked if I tried the sauce. He looked at me for a couple seconds in silence, then wished me luck.

What he failed to mention was that the peppers he made the sauce with were Carolina Reaper peppers. I had never put anything in my mouth that was anything close to that hot. It was like trying to swallow a red-hot piece of metal. I started sweating before I swallowed the first bite and took a sip of hot coffee, which only made it worse. I took another bite. Then another. I did not want to finish the eggs, but I could not stand letting food go to waste, so I powered through. About halfway into the eggs, I noticed everyone else had stopped eating and was watching me suffer. My face must have been beet red, but I finished all the eggs with tears in my eyes. I felt like a fish out of water when I set the fork down. The host looked a little shocked, then leaned back and said he was impressed. After I finished the eggs, he told me what was in the sauce.

I spent the next hour in the bathroom. When I came out, I felt a little better and did my morning chores before getting back on the road.

North from the hostel a couple hours was Forks, the town made famous by *The Twilight Saga*. I got off the main road and took some lazy detours through side streets to see what the town was like. The biggest disappointment was that I did not find any spoons, or forks for that matter.

I kept driving north, without any new eating utensils, and made it to Lake Pleasant. I sat on the side of the lake and pulled out my atlas. On it, I colored in the roads that I had been on in the last couple days and looked for my next stop. Cape Flattery is the most Northwestern point in the connected US, not counting the islands off its coast. It sounded like a good place to go next.

Highway 112 followed the northern coast before dropping south through a Native American Reservation and around to the cape. At the end of the road was a small parking lot and a trail leading to the edge of the cliffs. A sign at the trailhead informed readers about the area. Leaning against the sign was a bunch of walking sticks beside a donation box. I slipped a couple bucks in the box and grabbed a stick. I thought it would be a good idea to have a walking stick for the rest of the trip since many of the remaining states and provinces were mountainous and in bear country.

The trail ended on top of a steep cliff. The water below was breathtakingly blue-green, and the cliffs that made up the rest of the coast were intricately carved by years of waves violently crashing against them. A little less than a mile out from the viewpoint was Tatoosh Island and the Cape Flattery lighthouse. Across the ocean to the North, I could see Vancouver Island. I stayed there for a while, looking out at the ocean, and talking to an older bird-watching couple who were both photographers.

From Cape Flattery, I drove until I did not want to drive anymore. I made it through Port Angeles and started going south along the coast of the Puget Sound. I saw the sign for Deer Park and followed the road into the mountains where the road was suddenly closed off. This was unfortunate because I had to poop like no one's business, and the closest bathroom was at least 30 minutes away, back down the road. I grabbed my shovel tool from by backpack and some toilet paper and ran off into the trees to dig a hole. I did not want to drive right back down immediately, so I sat on a dirt ridge by the side of the road and started carving into the walking stick I had picked up. I cut rings into the top and bottom of the stick, then carved "PNW" for Pacific Northwest in bold letters into the middle of the stick.

After a couple hours hanging out in front of the closed gate, reading, writing, and carving, I drove back down the road and took the ferry from Kingston to Edmonds. The sun set as I crossed Puget Sound. I stood on the back of the ferry and watched the sky turn gold over Olympic National Park. Trees became silhouettes. The ocean glistened and sparkled brightly. Behind the trees, mountains stood tall and proud above the clouds with their peaks covered in snow. I had my camera around my neck and took dozens of photos of the ocean, the ferry, and the stunning mountains.

A Snapchat friend of mine lived in North Seattle and said that I should stay in Mukilteo if I was going to be sleeping in my van. I got off the ferry and found a shopping center in the city. I was tired from a long day of driving, and I was asleep as soon as my head hit the pillow.

The next day I texted my friend again and asked if she trusted any good chiropractors in the area. She said she went to one for sports injuries, one who works with a lot of high school athletes. She gave me the address, and I was on my way to Back to Health Chiropractic Center. The chiropractor was a cool dude and saw me immediately after I finished all the paperwork. I told him about what caused the injury, the symptoms, and the technique Hughes Chiropractic used to treat me. He told me it was no problem, laid me down, and snapped my neck back into place. He seemed shocked at how out of place it was. The hot grip loosened. My brain could breathe again. The fog retreated.

As with many unfortunate situations, my spinal injury is not completely a bad thing. The potential for my injury to be consuming is great and burns ever-present at the back of my mind. But where it has burned, it has cleared area for seeds to sprout. In order to know when I am not myself, I first have to know who I am. Being by myself in a van over a thousand miles away from where I grew up and from people I knew was the perfect opportunity for this kind of honesty.

After seeing someone else look back at me from that dirty Wal-Mart mirror in California, the road trip became so much less of a vacation. It became less about frolicking and more about finding my limits, pushing them, and learning about myself. I was getting to know that stranger in the mirror. As the cliché goes, the road trip became about the journey more than the destination.

To recognize my mental changes in new situations, I first had to know who I was in every situation. I had to be nothing but honest with myself, and that meant being honest with everyone I met. I could be nothing but kind to myself as I learned through the unfamiliar. Sometimes I made mistakes and had to forgive myself. As a result, I could be nothing but kind to other people because I could see that we all experience life new each day, making mistakes, learning, and needing forgiveness. From experience, I know a stern word or a slap to the face from a place of kindness can be effective. I came to realize, however, that harshness, anger, and retribution are largely unproductive. Only actions from compassion lift us to learn and grow. They inspire us to get back up when we fall.

Most of the morning remained when I left the chiropractor. I felt so much better and had the urge to look better too. I hadn't had a haircut since before I left on the trip, and my hair was getting thick, long, and shaggy. I again asked my friend for a recommendation. I wanted a good, cheap barber. She sent me to Nic's, home of the $8 haircut. The floor was checkered, and the waiting room had beer, TVs, and sports magazines. The back was open, and the barbers were incredible. I got the best haircut of my life. With a fresh cut and the ability to think in complete sentences, I felt like a new man by noon of my first day in Seattle.

Every day I was getting more and more excited to see Wilbur and Orville. We had made plans to go to a Life in Color show, a paint rave in Tacoma, Washington. We also hoped to do some hikes, walk around Seattle, and hang out in Olympic National Park. Their plane would land in a couple days, so I had to fill some time before they arrived. I needed to do some writing and to edit a lot of photos, tasks I had been putting off for a little too long.

I went to the Red Cup Café, which was very close to the Edmonds Port. I stayed there all day. It was on top a hill and had a view of Puget Sound and the mountains across the water. I sat on a bench covered in pillows and wrote and edited all day. I got there at brunch and stayed until they closed before dinner. It was busy around lunch and then again in the late afternoon. I usually didn't like to order food at cafes due to the expense, but I had also set aside some "treat yo self" money for Seattle. I got a few drinks and a few sandwiches and soups throughout the day.

The last hour I was in the café, I was researching tattoo parlors in Seattle. I knew at some point on the trip I wanted to get a tattoo, and I figured Seattle would be a good place to get one since it was about the halfway point and I would have my friends with me. I had no idea what I wanted, though. I called a few different places and found a place that looked good and had good reviews. I liked the artists' work.

I rushed to the shop in Seattle because it was late afternoon, and they were going to close. I met with an artist who had availability the next day and talked with him for a bit about the tattoo. I had no idea what I wanted, so I just spit balled some ideas with him. I wanted something to do with photography since it had come to mean so much to me and I knew I was going to continue with it. And I wanted a photo I had taken incorporated in the tattoo as well. I showed him a few photos I had taken the day before on the ferry. I also wanted the quote, "Tomorrow may never happen. Yesterday will never happen again," beneath the tattoo. It was a little mantra I had been living by while road tripping. It had kept me in the present and loving where I was, no matter where I was. He said he would come up with something that night.

I found myself with a few hours before Wilbur and Orville's plane was due to land. I needed to find something to do with all my excitement and energy. I drove around for an hour or so outside the city until I found a park with a long, paved walking trail that followed a river and the street. For the first time in a long time, I pulled my longboard out of the back and started riding. I pushed for miles in one direction. After the trail turned into more of a sidewalk, I turned around and pushed for several more miles back the way I had come until the paved walking trail started to end. Then, I sat down on my board and pushed with my hands for a few miles back the way I started. When I had reached the end again, the sky had turned to golden hour with increased energy in the air. I pushed back towards my van, still sitting. I passed a group of people walking dogs. As I sped by them, they cheered. A couple hundred feet later, I turned around again because I had passed my van. When I stood up to turn my board around, the group had gotten closer, and I could see their faces. They were shocked. I think when I had first passed them, they thought I was a paraplegic or had some other leg problems. One of them asked me why I was sitting and pushing with my hands. I gave her the deepest and truest answer I could think of: I don't know. Why not?

I stuck around in the parking lot after the sun went down and read until it was time to pick up Wilbur and Orville. I got to the airport right at the time they texted me to say they just touched down. I ran through the airport and found their gate right as they walked through the door. It was relieving and heart-filling to see those familiar faces. We hugged, and I took them back to my home. I had not really thought too far ahead, but sleeping with three people in the van was going to be interesting. We drove away from SEATAC, and the first thing we did was find a dispensary. Cannabis was newly legalized, and we wanted to bask in the legality. We all pitched in and got a couple sacks of some good bud and then found the closest Walmart. The two brothers wanted to see how I was living, so what a better way to start than sleeping in the back of a Walmart parking lot. We got stoned, then went to sleep. Somehow, we all fit in the same bed.

The next morning, we drove out to the Cascades to hike Rattlesnake Ledge. A surprising number of people were on the trail, but I was thrilled to hike with my best friends and show them a little bit of what my life looked like. The view from the top was amazing, and the hike through the thick woods was beautiful. I felt like I was a guide for Wilbur and Orville as we hiked up to Rattlesnake Ledge. Though I had never been to this mountain before, I had been going on hikes nearly every day for the last couple months, so it was less about showing them the mountain than guiding them through the life I had been living. About a month had passed since I last saw my brother. Short of that, I had mostly been meeting new people and telling the same stories about myself. With Wilbur and Orville, I could hear stories about what was happening in my hometown.

When we got back down, we went to Laughing Buddha for my tattoo appointment, but when we got there, the artist said he was not going to be able to do it. The said the client he had before me was "being a little bitch." The client was getting a small tattoo on his back and had already passed out twice. He told me to come back at the same time the next day, and he would fit me in. The tattoo delay was probably for the best because that night, Wilbur, Orville, and I were going down to Tacoma for the rave. Raving and getting covered in paint would not have been the best idea with a fresh tat. Since we were already in the city, we walked around downtown, went to Starbucks Reserve, and got some phenomenal drinks. After that and exploring the Space Needle, we drove down to Tacoma and checked into the cheapest motel we could find. We figured a shower would be needed after the rave. We couldn't shower in the van.

The rave was crazy. We got to the venue in the evening and waited in a line that stretched down the block. We were crossfaded by the time we got through the doors, and we danced for hours. Paint sprayed from the stage, and rave-goers could buy packets of paint to throw around. By the time we left at one in the morning, we were exhausted and soaked to the bone with paint and sweat. The shower that night was incredible.

Slightly hungover the next morning, we drove back to Seattle for my tattoo. This time, the artist was waiting for me. He flashed the drawing he had made. I gave it the thumbs up, and we went up to his studio. This was my first tattoo, and it was large with a lot of shading. The image was a camera based on the camera I had at the time. In the camera lens was an outline of the mountains in Olympic National Park from a photo I had taken on the ferry to Seattle. The tattoo took a little over three hours to finish. I was told it might hurt, but the pain was not too bad. I got the tattoo on my thigh where I had a lot of meat. The shading on the more-sensitive bottom and backside of my thigh was the most painful.

Tattoo finished, we piled back in the van and took the ferry back across Puget Sound to Olympic. We had no plans for where exactly we were going. We just wanted to camp somewhere. I suggested a spot I drove past a few days before: Seal Rock. It was a campground right on the water overlooking Puget Sound with a view of Mount Rainier. At a store just up the road, we stocked up on beer, firewood, and food for three days of camping. The first night we had a big fire, cooked some hot dogs, and drank a lot of beer. I kept looking at my tattoo. It was cool, but it was going to be weird getting used to seeing a big black piece of art on my leg for the rest of my life.

Because three people in a van get a little cramped, I set up my hammock at our site. The night turned too chilly for hammock sleeping, though, so, we all ended up in the van for the night again. We had an unspoken agreement that the two people on the sides would sleep on their sides facing out, and the middle person would sleep on his back. With extra bodies, the uninsulated van was warm for a change.

We woke up around 11 and made a little coffee and a breakfast of sweet rolls. We spent the day enjoying the outdoors, sitting around a fire, smoking, and drinking on the beach, and hanging with our favorite Aunt Lucy. My leg was healing from the tattoo, and we were still tired from the rave. We didn't leave the campsite the whole day.

We had talked a few times about going further into the park if it was open. We hoped to find a trail and see if we could hike 10-15 miles, but that didn't end up happening. We woke up late the next day, still tired, so we decided to spend our last full day at the campsite. I realized I missed being around familiar people. During the last few weeks far away from home and in the company of strangers, I hadn't felt like I missed anyone. I was busy living one day at a time, and my days were full. I did not want to go back to Missouri or Illinois. I was away from the Midwest and had no desire to return. Outside of my family and the familiarity, I didn't see the Midwest as home.

We went back to the store up the road and got some more food for the day. Then we spent the day sitting either on the rocky beach or at the campsite. We mostly just caught up with each other, shot the shit, and solved world problems. I was grateful for the break in all the strangeness I had on the trip recently. Having my best friends come to see me on the west coast made it easier to keep going. After a couple months on the road, roaming in a van started to feel like just the normal thing to do. But seeing my best friends made me think of our shared childhoods playing football in the streets, running to and from each-others houses, and getting Sunny-D and Pop-Tarts from Wilbur and Orville's house while we waited for the school bus to pick us up. Time with them made me more excited about what I was doing.

As the days disappeared, the time came to do something else that had become part of my new normal: saying goodbye. The Wright boys had to fly out to go back to work and school, and I had to continue up the coast to cross the Canadian border. This goodbye was a lot easier than some of the others because I knew I would be seeing them again soon and that we'd have a lot of stories to tell over a few beers and joints. I dropped them off at the Sea-Tac airport in the afternoon, and I turned North again.

One of the places I was told to go see was Anacortes on Fidalgo Island. I found a campsite near the ocean and paid for a site. I had stopped at a lot more campsites than I thought I would. It was nice to have a fire and sit outside in the evenings.

I walked down the hill from the campsite towards the ocean a little before sunset with my camera slung over my shoulder. At the end of the road coming out of the camp where the road came to a T, I found an opening through the brush onto the beach. I pushed a branch aside and walked down onto the rocky shore. I was on an archipelago. Across a stretch of ocean, was another island covered in dark green conifer trees. Golden hour was starting, and the farthest tree-covered island I could see was swallowing the sun before it reached the horizon. I made my way slowly along the shore until I came to a fallen tree. On the other side of the tree was an older man standing on the beach.

I wasn't really in the mood to talk to anyone. I was feeling a little peopled out for the day. But he wanted to talk, so I indulged him and listened. We stood and watched the sunset while we talked. He asked a lot about what I was doing out here, where I was from, and a lot of questions about my travels thus far. He was from Idaho. Well, he lived in Idaho but was from Everett, Washington. He and his wife used to come to Anacortes and take ferries around the islands to explore. It was one of their favorite things to do. His wife died a couple years ago, so once a year he would come out to Anacortes, camp for a couple days, and watch the ferries leave the port. He couldn't bring himself to get on the ferries for a day trip to one of the islands without her, so now he just watched them go. He told me some more about his wife and the places they had gone and then fell quiet for a while as the sun continued to drop into the islands on the horizon. I think he was a little embarrassed because he thought he shared too much, or maybe he just felt like he needed to move. Right after the peak colors of sunset passed, he quickly excused himself and went back to the campsite through the brush.

I unslung my camera from my shoulder and took a few photos as the light of the day was fading. I laid the Tamron lens I had bought the month before on a tree while I swapped to my 50mm prime lens. As soon as I snapped the lens in, I heard a very faint scrape, like the sound of plastic sliding on wood. I turned just in time to see the lens fall from the tree, bounce twice on rocks, and splash into a shallow tidal pool. I lunged for the lens and grabbed it after it had been in the water for only a second, but it was already too late. I could see seawater inside the lens. That hurt. I had barely used the lens during the month I owned it. Had I not bought it, I could have saved more money for food. I was furious with myself for not setting the lens on the ground.

The Tamron had been my widest-angle lens. Now I was down to the 50mm, which isn't very wide, as my widest-angle lens. I had been using wider lenses for most of my landscape shots since they were able to capture so much of the beautiful mountain surroundings. Now I was a day away from going into Canada, and I would not be able to capture the grandeur of the Garibaldis or the Canadian Rockies. I had no clue how I was going to get good landscape shots with a 50mm lens. It was the wrong lens, and I wasn't a good enough photographer yet to attempt using it for the shots I wanted. I thought I was fucked, and I started to give up on thinking about bringing my camera on my Canadian hikes. What was the point if I couldn't get the shots I wanted?

In the morning, I was still a little pissed about dropping the lens in the water. I looked up an oil and lube place to get my second oil change of the trip. Over 6,000 miles of road were behind me. I decided it wasn't so bad. If the lens was the worst thing to happen so far in 6,000 crazy miles.

With fresh oil and a full tank of gas, I made it to the Canadian border. I was ready to pull off to the side and be questioned because I assumed a young man living in a van crossing international borders would warrant a lot of questions about his intentions in Canada, but the border agent let me in after surprisingly few questions. I just had to promise that I was not going to stay and live in Canada and that I would be back in America in less than a couple months.

I knew it wasn't going to be that easy going back into America

12. Sea to Sky

After I crossed the Canadian border, I skirted around Vancouver and got on the Sea to Sky Highway, perhaps the most beautiful drive in British Columbia. The highway begins just north of Vancouver and follows the coast for the first hour or so until it turns into the mountains to end at Pemberton, just North of Whistler. I had already reserved a bed in the HI Whistler Hostel for the night.

I arrived at the hostel early in the afternoon, carrying a backpack with a couple changes of clothes into the hostel at check in. Everything else, I left in the van.

I met an English guy named Will who was in the bunk above me. We chatted for a bit after I put my stuff in the locker at the foot of the bed. Before I left the hostel, we planned to invite the rest of the room to a brewery that night. I was stoked to go out in British Columbia; I could use my real ID since the drinking age was not as stupidly high as it is in America.

Across from the hostel parking was a bridge over a gushing river. A trail ran along both sides of the river. I walked along one side for a couple miles until I came to a bridge, and I returned on the other trail. I had the day to kill, and the trail was easy. I took my time, played in the river, and meditated on some rocks to the sound of white water. The afternoon was perfect.

After a can of soup in the hostel kitchen, I met up with Will, but no one else from our room joined us. We arrived at Whistler Brewing Company a little before sunset. I had been to the brewery the year before. Eager to revisit good memories, I looked for and found my favorite beer there: Bear Paw Honey Lager. For every other round of drinks, I would have a pint of the delicious lager.

Will and I chatted about life, what we were doing in Canada, and things we should do before leaving. He was a financial advisor looking at moving to Canada in the next year or two, so he was scouting jobs and locations. We started talking about sports and found we both wanted to try mountain biking while we were in Whistler. The hostel had mountain bikes we could rent for $10 for the day, so we made plans to rent some bikes and find some trails the next morning.

We bought each other round after round until we were piss drunk and the bar gave a last call. He wanted to get on a bus to go into Whistler to get some cigarettes. I wanted to go to bed, so we split up. I stumbled the mile-long trail back to the hostel alone.

My hangover the next morning was rough, but at 9:00, I got out of bed, showered, ate a Pop-Tart in my van, and met Will in the lobby to rent bikes. We went out the back of the hostel and onto a dirt path that led to the forest. Neither of us had looked at a map or asked anyone for trail recommendations, so we just explored. We found a good bike trail that was hard in some spots, but we managed. Eventually the trail climbed steeper and turned onto an old logging road. We followed that for a while until it ended and turned back into a small foot-trail that went up the mountain. We biked up a steep section, around in a large half circle, to the top of an avalanche path of huge rocks.

Will and I looked at each other, said fuck it, and started biking down the boulders. He took the lead. Following him down boulders on a bike was one of the sketchiest things I had done thus far. I had no mountain bike experience, and this route would have been difficult for anyone. I got maybe halfway down, going slowly, before I missed a several-foot drop to the boulder below. I rode off the rock, squeezed the front brake, stopped abruptly when I landed, and went over my handlebars. I tumbled down a couple boulders like a ragdoll. I tore the hell out of my elbows, forearms, and some of my side. I also sprained my wrist again.

By the time I stood up to make sure I was still in one piece, Will had made it to the bottom of the boulder section. Carrying a heavy mountain bike a few hundred feet down more boulders sounded worse than riding, so I scrambled up the rocks to get back on my bike. I eased the rest of the way down. Soon after the boulders, we stopped at a small stream by the trail to refill our water bottles. I washed the blood off of me. After years of snowboarding, I had become accustomed to wrist sprains and other injuries, so I could manage biking back with a sprained wrist. It wasn't fun, but miles away from civilization and halfway up a mountain, we didn't have many options to get back to the hostel.

A mile from the hostel, Will stopped and said he thought one of the trails that split off went to an old train wreck. We followed a trail that looked promising and eventually came to the wreck. Many years ago, the train was derailed, and the boxcars are still strewn around the woods. They were covered in graffiti, and bikers had turned some of the boxcars into features to jump off or onto. We explored the cars for an hour before going back to the hostel.

Once again, I had a braced wrist. For the rest of the day, I hung out in the hostel lounge, wrote a little bit for a blog post, and swiped on Tinder in hopes of meeting a local. I matched with a woman from Pemberton, and we started talking a bit. In my bio, I shared that I was traveling around looking for fun things to do and cool things to see. I had also mentioned that I was photographer.

The woman's name was June, and she was free for the following day. She wanted to do a photoshoot because she really enjoyed modeling and trying new shots with beginning photographers. She asked what type of shoot I wanted to try, and I mentioned that boudoir, especially outdoors, would be cool. She said she knew of a few waterfalls we could check out. We agreed to meet up the next afternoon.

After June and I finalized plans, I drove to the base of Whistler to check out the resort town and hikes. I walked around the shops for a bit and then ran into Will who said he was going to a cigar store that sold pipes and pieces to smoke out of. I tagged along and got a dugout from the place. I had never heard of a dugout before, but it seemed like the perfect thing to have for a quick smoke by myself on hikes or in a hammock.

We walked around the Whistler base a bit and then around on some trails. The hangover and rough bike adventure were still kicking our asses a little, so we wanted to take it easy. About a mile into the walk, we came to a popular lake that was a perfect spot on a nice day. We sat there for an hour or so. Will said a few people from the hostel were getting drinks later that night. I didn't want to try driving back if I drank as much as I did the night before. I wanted to drive the van back to the hostel and return to Whistler base on the bus after dinner. We headed back to my van.

In the parking lot, I found my van, but there was a problem. The rear driver's side tire was popped from a hole in the sidewall. I had a spare tire in the back of the van, but it was not easy to get to. For more than an hour, I swapped the tires out. I would have to buy a new tire soon because I did not want to be driving another few thousand miles through the mountains without a spare.

I think we drank as much as we did the night before. This time we visited two bars and broke the drinking up with some bar food. I don't remember getting back to the hostel. I woke up in my hostel bed. I showered and said goodbye to Will. The other two staying in the room had already gone by the time I woke up.

I read by a river until about an hour before I was supposed to meet up with June. Before heading her way, I went back to Whistler Brewing Co and bought a couple six-packs of Bear Paw. I drank a pint of the porter they had on tap to calm my nerves. I had never done a boudoir shoot before. Hell, I had never seen a woman in lingerie in person before, much less a total stranger I met on Tinder the day before. Down the road from the brewery, at a pull-off, I met up with June. She was chipper, excited for the shoot, and had a large bag stuffed with different outfits.

When meeting new people, especially Tinder dates in cities, I found it was best if I didn't drive, even if that meant getting into a stranger's car. People seemed more at ease and opened up more when they knew I trusted them.

June drove us to Rainbow Falls, and we started up the trail. I thought I was in pretty good shape and a fast hiker, but June was a mountain goat. I struggled to keep up with her. We reached the end of the trail with a view of the falls. I took a few photos of her on a rock near the bottom of the falls, and then we started walking slowly down the trail, looking for what might be a good spot in the forest to do some boudoir photos.

Up to that point, we hadn't seen anyone else, so we settled on a spot not too far off the trail. She stripped down and went through some poses. I didn't have much going for me on this shoot, and that's one of the reasons I was so nervous to do it. I mean, I was buzzed, unfamiliar with the location, had just met this incredibly beautiful and now scantily clad woman, and I wasn't used to the lens I was using. That being said, I think I did a pretty good job, and the photos turned out much better than I thought they would.

After I showed her some of the photos on my camera and she got dressed, she said we should check out the next spot. We went back down the trail, got in her car, and drove down the highway to Brandywine Falls. Past the viewing area for the falls was a fence that June told me to jump over. I was a little hesitant, but she seemed to know what she was doing, so I hopped over, and she followed. We scrambled down the mountain, wove our way through the trees, and ended up at the bottom of the falls with an incredible view.

June was a cool person. She told me about a lot of amazing places and things to do in British Columbia and Vancouver Island. She had quite the story about traveling and living with health problems. While we climbed back up the mountain, she told me about Whistler Bungee, a bungee jumping place on a bridge not too far from Brandywine Falls. More specifically she told me about a little-known promotion. If you jumped naked, the jump was free. Needless to say, getting naked and jumping off a bridge quickly went to the top of my BC to-do list.

When June dropped me back off at my van, I drove back to the Brandywine parking lot and walked down a different trail to look for Whistler Bungee. I found it, but it was closed for the day.

I drove back to Pemberton, and walked to Nairn Falls, a waterfall just South of town. A campground lies downstream of the falls. I didn't have a place to sleep for the night. Evening was settling, so I got a campsite right above the river for a couple days.

In the morning, I drove up to Joffre Provincial Park and started on the trail. It followed a stream up a mountain, starting at the lower lake, going around to a middle lake, and ended at the upper lake. Joffre was one of my favorite hikes. The trail was strenuous, and the views amazed me. I was tempted to jump in the middle lake, but ice still covered it. I should have jumped in. Instead, I returned to the van exhausted and drove around on back country roads. I got lost for a few hours. Darkness had fallen by the time I got back to my site at Nairn.

The morning greeted me with a light fog that stuck around for a while. I didn't want to do anything. I was in one of the best campgrounds I had ever camped at, just downstream from a roaring waterfall. Everything was alive and moving, but I felt an amazing calmness, like I was one with everything. I drove down the street to One Mile Lake on the edge of Pemberton. For a couple hours I walked around the lake and ducked beneath tree branches during short bouts of rain. I snapped photos as I walked, trying to get used to the 50mm lens that I was now stuck with as my primary lens. I had taken some photos at Joffre, but few of the photos turned out like I wanted.

When I was satisfied with my photographic outing, I returned to camp for the day and heated up some soup. The new stove really changed the soup making game. It was a small, collapsible stove that screwed onto the top of a propane can. It had ridges that held a can of soup perfectly, and it only took a couple minutes until the soup was almost boiling. After I ate, I walked back to the waterfall and found a good rock. I sat on it and read.

Sitting and reading on a rock with background music of the gushing river, sipping a honey lager, I truly fell in love with life. This was exactly what I wanted to do and what I wanted life to be. I could sit on top of a rock, read a good book, get lost in the rapids, tend to a fire beneath low hanging clouds drifting through green pine boughs, and everything would be as it was supposed to be. Everything was perfect.

I think what happened is that I truly appreciated my autonomy, and I think that's something a lot of people struggle with. I recognized that every decision I made was mine to make. I bore the full responsibility for all my actions, and I had the sole power to choose my path. Any bad thing that happened to me was a result of my decisions. Anything good that happened to me was a result of my decisions. If I was unhealthy, it was because of my diet or my lifestyle. If I was happy, it was because I chose to be happy and to do things that led to more happiness.

I knew I would walk away from this bliss the next day. I wasn't looking forward to it.

Half of me wanted to skip the drive down to Vancouver, to skip over Vancouver altogether. Lea, an old girlfriend, was in Vancouver. Even thinking about being in the same city as her gave me anxiety.

We had seen each other the year before. When I visited her in Vancouver, the visit had not gone well. I still felt like she was the one who got away. She left the Midwest for Vancouver after she graduated high school. Not long afterwards, I had the accident that turned my world upside down. We had been keeping in contact until after I visited her at UBC. While I was with her, I was not me. I was not who I should have been. I would like to blame the dumpster fire our relationship became on my injury, but blaming everything on my injury doesn't feel fair. In truth, I fucked everything up with us.

I drove the van into the city where Lea still lived. As soon as I got into downtown Vancouver, I think I had another anxiety attack. It was not as bad as the one I had in Oregon, but I certainly had a hard time driving. I was in a huge, busy city with no idea how to navigate. My feet kept bouncing on the pedals. I had been trying to stay out of cities for the most part, but I had booked a hostel right in the middle of downtown Vancouver because I wanted to party with travelers for a few days. The hostel I booked was surrounded by a lot of clubs and bars. I found the hostel, but I couldn't find parking. Few parking garages within a mile would fit my van, and the ones that did charged $30 per day. I was not going to pay that.

I called the hostel to cancel my reservation and then sat in a grocery store parking lot on the edge of the city for 20 minutes. It was late afternoon, and I wanted to do the same thing I did in Oregon: drive. I wanted to drive for hours. . . far away from Vancouver. I didn't want to be there, I had to get out. I needed to go. I didn't like cities, and the fact that Lea was there reminded me how much I screwed up. I needed to leave that second.

Instead, gripping the wheel with white knuckles, I broke down and called Lea. There was no one else to call.

To my surprise, she answered the phone. Lea told me not to leave before exploring Vancouver. She said it was a wonderful city and suggested a hostel on Jericho Beach that was probably cheaper than the one downtown, perhaps with parking, too.

When she hung up, I drove to Jericho. Only for one night, though. I would leave first thing in the morning. I wanted to see and experience Vancouver, but my stomach was in knots. Leaving the city would be the only way to untie those knots. I checked in to the hostel when I probably should have just slept on the side of the road.

Though it was only dinner time, I laid down on starched sheets in a room with 39 other beds and faced the wall to try and sleep. This didn't really seem like a hostel for travelers, but rather a hostel for people who had nowhere else to go. I felt like I fit in.

"Hey man, "said an Irish accent. You're new. Where are you from?"

"Hey dude," I said half-heartedly. "Yeah, I'm from Missouri, America. I'm on a road trip." I didn't open my eyes or roll over to face him.

"Tight dude. I'm from Ireland." The voice persisted, "Why are you laying down so early? Are you tired or something?"

"Not really. I'm just not in that great a headspace right now, and I don't really want to do anything," I explained so he would go away and let me be.

"Oh, well okay," he said to my relief. I thought he would leave. But then he kept talking, "If you want to do something to get your mind off whatever it is, there are a few Germans in the kitchen who are really, really stoned. I cooked them a bunch of spaghetti. They're so high, man. They're kind of struggling to eat, and their English is really broken." Still, he kept talking, "It's kind of funny to try and figure what they're saying. You're welcome to join. I'll introduce you to people."

"I'm about to go back there," he said to my relief. He continued, "I think there's some leftover spaghetti if you're hungry. Want to join?"

I didn't want to get up. I wanted him to leave me alone, but I knew I probably should do something. Sitting in the dark in a 40-bed bunkroom wasn't going to do me much good anyway. I said, "I guess, sure. Thanks." I swung my legs over the side of the bed and put my feet in my boots.

"I'm Ian," Ian said with his hand extended when I stood up.

"Alex," I replied. "How long have you been here?" I shook Ian's hand and started following him into the hallway and down the stairs to the kitchen.

"A couple weeks. I've been traveling around Canada a little bit, and my visa is about to expire. I'm spending my last month overseas here in Van City," he said.

We got down to the kitchen, and Ian was right. Three Germans sat around one massive bowl of spaghetti. Even from halfway across the room, I could see how stoned they were. People from all over the world filled the rest of the long wooden table.

Ian and I sat down. He introduced me to everyone. Meeting so many new people was a much welcome distraction for me. I immediately felt lighter. We all joked around until the Germans finished their pasta. Then we went out on the front porch of the hostel to smoke a joint before playing card games in the lounge.

The next day I walked. I had decided to stay at least another day because I was excited to explore the city. The hostel was a few miles away from downtown Vancouver. Plenty of busses ran to the city center, but I needed to walk. I was low on funds and needed to start watching money carefully. Gas was very expensive in Canada, and I still needed to buy a new tire.

I walked around Kitsilano Beach, over across the Granville Bridge to downtown, went into Stanley Park, and on to the Lion's Gate Bridge. Then I looped back around the Seawall, zig zagged through the West End, went up and down another few city streets, found a dispensary downtown, bought some bud, walked back through Kitsilano, and finally found my way through some neighborhoods back to the hostel. After twenty-two miles, I was exhausted.

I played cards with Ian and one of the other guys from our pod of bunk beds. We made plans to go to the University of British Columbia's campus on the end of the peninsula to check out Wreck Beach the next day. I went to bed and woke up to the sound of someone throwing up in bed a few pods down. I woke up again at 7. The room woke up at 7 because someone's alarm went off, beeping for ten straight minutes.

I went out to make coffee at my van and then started researching to see if it was possible to get my damaged camera lens fixed. I didn't have much hope since salt water had been in the lens, but I figured it would be worth a shot. I walked four miles to a shop I found online and dropped off the lens. The guy said he'd look at it but seemed doubtful.

It was afternoon when I got back to the hostel and met up with the others to walk down to UBC. On the way, we stopped by a liquor store for bottles of wine.

We got to the university, went down Main Mall to the Rose Garden and walked around campus a little to look at all the gorgeous buildings. In the past, I had looked into maybe going to school at UBC. It felt kind of weird being there. It was slightly familiar and brought back memories of Lea from the year before. The whole time I was on the campus, in her space with my hostel friends, I felt like something was off. I was glad I was intoxicated.

We descended the steep stairs that went on forever from campus to Wreck Beach and found a spot in the sand. We joined in a frisbee game and then settled on a spot against a log to drink our wine while the sun set.

I brought my camera along to keep trying to get used to the 50mm. My shots form Wreck Beach turned out better than I thought they would, and I was able to capture what I wanted to capture. I was starting to feel more comfortable with the forced change in photography style. Or maybe it wasn't a change of style; maybe it was the beginning of creating my style. My initial style was mostly just wide-angle landscape shots with minimal framing. It didn't take much thought, mostly just point-and-shoot after I got the settings dialed in. Being stuck with the 50mm, I had to think about what angle I wanted, where I had to stand, and what specific part of the landscape I wanted to focus on.

Drunk, we walked in the dark to the bus stop in front of campus to catch a ride to our hostel at Jericho Beach. We passed out as soon as our heads hit the pillows.

I decided to spend one last full day in Vancouver. I walked to Vanier Park and smoked out of my new dugout while I sat on a bench looking out across the inlet to the massive buildings of Granville Island. The smoke rejuvenated me a little, and I wanted to do some more walking.

I turned around and followed the coast back down all the way to Wreck Beach. The year before, I had done nude yoga there, and I wanted to do it again. Clothing is optional, and plenty of people take advantage of the opportunity. I got there, found a little area away from the larger group of people, and went through some yoga poses. I got sand in places I didn't even know were places, but it was worth it.

Nude yoga is one of the most freeing thigs you can do. Especially on a BC beach. After I finished, I went over to a log close to the water and sat on it, smoking a little more from my dugout. A naked dude was walking down the beach yelling, "Banana Bread! Anyone want banana bread?" He was carrying a full loaf. He walked up to me and asked if I wanted a piece, but I didn't have any money because, well, I didn't have pockets in my birthday suit. I offered a couple hits from my dugout as a trade, and he agreed. The banana bread was homemade, and it was very good.

I stayed on the beach until sunset before walking to the bus stop and catching a ride to the hostel. My legs were dead from walking on asphalt and concrete for so many miles the last few days. I needed to get back out to the mountains and dirt. I needed to continue my adventure. It was my last night at the hostel, so the friends I had made who were still around got together and had a couple drinks and a couple joints on the beach.

I checked out in the late morning and drove over to the camera place to see if my lens was salvageable. When I dropped it off, I had told the guy I left it with that I was going to pick it up this morning. When I showed up for it, I learned that my lens was still totally taken apart, sitting in pieces since the day before. There was no saving it, so I directed for it to be put it back together and sent to my home address in Missouri.

From there, I drove east. I had already gone west as far as I could go. Then I had traveled north along the Pacific coast until I hit the farthest northwest I was going to go, the farthest from home I would be on this trip. I felt pretty good about what I had done to this point. Turning east signified the beginning of the last, long leg of the journey. I began to worry I wouldn't be able to do everything I had originally wanted to do because of my dwindling funds, but I pushed that thought to the back of my head.

It was berry season in the Okanagan valley, and I passed several berry stands and orchards before I finally pulled over to buy some fresh berries and cherries to snack on for the next couple days. When I reached Penticton, I pulled into Skaha Lake Park to start researching wineries to visit. Around Okanagan Lake, wineries seemed to sit at least on every block, and vineyards covered the hills. I settled on going to Perseus Winery. I tasted a lot of wine and bought a Cab Sauvé and a few bottles of Resiling. When I learned the Resiling had won the Patio Pounder Award, I was instantly sold on it. A delicious wine easy to slam is my favorite type of wine.

From the winery, I went into the mountains to find a hike and a good spot to hammock for the rest of the day. I came across an ATV path and parked at the pull-off next to a couple trucks. I packed my normal bag, this time also with my dugout to smoke while I hiked. I was starting to truly become a hippy, and I was stoked about that. My hair was getting longer. I was hammocking more, smoking more, and life was feeling groovy.

After about a mile of walking and a few puffs, a small rock ledge started alongside the trail. I took another puff and walked along on top of the ledge. From the top of the little ledge, I had a birds-eye view of Okanagan Lake at the base of the mountain. Stoned, I was lost in thought while walking on the ledge, looking at the lake. After a while, I looked over to the trail. To my surprise, the ledge had had gotten significantly steeper and taller. The ATV path was probably about twelve feet below me now. I stopped to look back. I wanted to get off the ledge and return to the trail. I was also surprised to see that for at least a few hundred feet behind and in front of me, the ledge was at least ten feet or higher above the trail.

The smart thing to do would have been to either try and climb down or to walk back the way I had come until I found a safe space to get down, but I decided to jump. My wrist was still in a brace from falling off the mountain bike, but apparently that wasn't enough of a reminder not to do anything stupid.

Between the bottom of the small cliff I was on and the trail was a shallow ditch. All I had to do was clear that couple feet of ditch, and I could land flat on the grassy trail. I've fallen many times from snowboarding, biking, skateboarding, and doing general life stuff. If there's one thing I know, it's how to fall. In fact, just the year before, I had accidentally snowboarded off a cliff on the Whistler glacier in a white-out snowstorm and didn't even know I was off the cliff until I landed hard and sank up to my nipples in powder. I ended up okay then, so I would be okay jumping off this cliff too. Right?

As I leapt off the ledge, the ground beneath my foot crumbled. What was supposed to be a small jump ended up being an uncontrolled fall. I hit the ground hard, half in the ditch. I laid still for a few moments, stood up, and, after a few pats and slow movements, discovered I was totally fine. I didn't even have minor scrapes or bruises. I got lucky

I figured I had pushed my luck enough for the day. I went off the trail and up the mountain until I found a couple trees that would fit a hammock between them. The spot had a view of the lake. I spent all afternoon reading, smoking, and swaying between the trees. I stayed until early evening when I walked back to the van to get ready for bed.

I slept in and spent the morning swiping on Tinder while eating a couple granola bars. I made plans with a woman, April, to climb a mountain that night on the other side of the lake. After breakfast I hopped between little lakeside parks along the shore, stopping to write and edit photos.

April had pushed back the time we were meeting, so I didn't arrive at the base of the mountain we were going to climb until an hour before sunset. When we met at the trailhead, we each had a water bottle, a bottle of wine, and some snacks. She brought cheese and crackers, and I brought berries. Halfway up the paved trail, darkness fell, and the wind gusted. The top of the mountain was bitterly cold, so we backtracked to a picnic table a quarter mile down the trail to drink and eat.

We talked a lot about life and travels, and we each finished the bottle we brought plus all the food. I honestly don't remember too much about April She seemed like a lot of fun, but I only saw her for a couple hours. We were drinking most of that time. We stumbled down the trail well after midnight and said our goodbyes. From where I had parked in front of someone's house, I rolled myself up like a burrito in the van and passed out. I slept better than I had in a week. I hadn't slept well since Whistler, probably due to my nerves about Vancouver. But that night, drunk at the base of the mountain after coming in from the cold, I slept like a rock.

The sun woke me up early since I didn't close the curtains. I had a long drive to Jasper National Park ahead of me, so it was a good thing I got an early start. I passed through Kamloops and then went northeast towards Jasper. Encroaching upon the border of Alberta, Mount Robson peered down upon the road and towered above the mountains next to it. The country had turned from grassy and forested mountains into snow-capped, Rocky Mountains spiking out of lush pine forest. The air was clean and sweet. I pulled off at a scenic viewpoint and stared up at the view of Mount Robson while I ate my granola bar and berry lunch. That area might have been the most majestic and beautiful place I had ever been.

My spirit felt full again. I was excited. I was happy. I felt at peace and ready to explore new and beautiful country.

13. Icefields Parkway

"Good heavens, put your willy away!" came a woman's shriek in a heavy British accent.

Multiple pairs of feet walking through leaves, and hasty, drunken Canadian apologies followed.

I was sitting on the hard, wooden picnic bench beside the dancing flames in my fire pit. Earlier in the night I had cracked open a bottle of the patio pounder wine I picked up from Perseus. I had opened it only to taste it, but true to its name, it was too easy to pound. I had finished it all quickly, drinking straight from the bottle.

In the campsite next to me, three tipsy British women on holiday sat around a fire. Next to them was a parked trailer and four Canadians from Edmonton. One of the men had gotten too drunk and had wandered away from his site to take a piss. He either forgot where the bathroom was or was simply too drunk to care, but he ended up whipping his dick out and pissing on the edge of the British women's campsite in full light of their fire. His friends got him and dragged him back to their campsite after the British women yelled. I think they could hear me laughing. The women said they didn't want to see dicks on vacation; they were all nurses and had seen plenty. They didn't want to be reminded of work.

After waking up and making a pot of coffee, I started driving in the direction of Malign Lake. On the way to the lake, several cars in front of me pulled over to the shoulder very quickly, so I did the same. Other people were getting out of their cars, so I hopped out of the van and grabbed my camera. I figured there must be a big animal somewhere. I was right. A hundred feet behind me and down a steep hill, a chunky black bear was taking a stroll. This was the first wild bear I had ever seen. It was big and beautiful, lumbering up the hill toward the cars. It was a thick bear; he had been eating well that summer. As he walked in my general direction, I was practically holding the shutter of my camera down, snapping dozens of photos. I checked through some of the photos and made some adjustments to the settings. When I looked back up, the bear was barely more than twenty feet from me, and still coming my way.

The bear and I held eye contact while I slowly backed up and around my van to the driver's door. When I put my hand on the handle, a black, furry faced peered around the back of my van. His body was touching the van, and I could hear him breathe. We held eye contact for what felt like a full minute. Then he sniffed at me, gave me a neutral look, turned, and crossed the street into the forest. It had been a while since I had showered, but I didn't know I smelled too bad for a bear's standards.

I parked at Malign Lake and was awestruck when I walked to the shore. It was every bit as beautiful as it looked in photos. Wanting to get away from the many people by the boathouse on the shore closest to the parking lot, I found a trail and followed it through the woods, skirting the lake. After a couple miles I saw a huge boulder jutting out onto the lake that looked like a beautiful place to eat lunch.

I made my way to it and climbed up. I was above a lot of the trees on the shore but still felt tiny looking up at the snowy mountains. I took my time, nibbling at the granola bar, taking in as much of the scenery as I could.

I should have kept a photo journal of the best places I ate lunch. On most every hike, I tried to find the most beautiful part to stop for lunch. Every day I wanted to dedicate some time to enjoying the natural world around me and being wholly present in the moment. Looking out at waterfalls, canyons, valleys, mountains, deserts, or lakes was the best way to get the most out of wherever I was. Intentionally stopping was also a way to make sure I ate and consumed needed calories every day, something I had gotten bad at.

After the hike, I was even sweatier and smellier than I was when the bear left me alone. More than a week had passed since I showered, and even I was put off by my body odor. I figured a glacial lake would make for a good bath. I hadn't seen public showers anywhere in the town of Jasper, so I followed a sign to Pyramid Lake for a swim.

The sky was overcast. When I found a place to park near the lake, it smelled like rain would come soon. The temperature was in the low 50's, and even though it was the beginning of June, snow still dotted the shore. I knew the water was going to be frigid, but it would also be so incredibly refreshing. I changed into swim trunks and walked up to my calves in the freezing lake. I took a breath, sprinted through the shallows, and dove. My body went numb as soon as I hit the water, but I took a few powerful butterfly strokes to warm up, then flipped on my back to kick gently back to the shore.

The water was cold, but the shock had worn off by the time I flipped onto my back. I shivered, but every part of my body felt awake and alert. Plus, I probably didn't smell as repulsive. When I floated back to the shallows, I sat on the pebble floor of the lake to catch my breath.

Rain fell in heavy droplets from the heavens. The rain was warmer than the lake, so it felt like a warm shower. I laid in the water, flat on my back, and let the rain splash down on me until it stopped fifteen minutes later. It was the best shower of my entire life, and certainly the best of the trip. I didn't take many nice showers. Most of my showers were in public showers, campgrounds, or truck stops. Some were free. Some cost a few dollars. But that rain shower made up for every three-dollar, luke-warm truck-stop shower.

Van life was full of tradeoffs. Almost every day required a sacrifice of modern amenities and comforts like a private bathroom, shower, kitchen, or heater. I woke up at 4 a.m. with trucks starting in the next parking space over. I had to sleep in multiple layers because I didn't have insulation in the van. I usually had no idea where I was going to sleep that night, and I had to clean inside the van constantly. Traveling in a van was not always ideal. Almost none of it was ideal. But occasionally, everything lined up and created an amazing experience I could never forget, and all the less-than-ideal experiences slipped away. I wouldn't have traded the

Pyramid Lake rain shower for anything. It made me all the more grateful to be living as a nomad.

I pulled back into my campsite feeling like a new person. The RV housing the British women was gone. The Canadians were drinking beers and sitting around their fire. I made a meal on the picnic table, and I was about to light a fire in the fire pit when one of the Canadians walked over. He invited me to join them for some card games and drinks if I wanted.

I gratefully followed him over and played card games with the four of them. They gave me a couple beers, too. When it got too dark to see the cards outside, we packed into their small trailer and played more card games. They were from a rural town around Edmonton and were vacationing for the weekend. They asked me a lot of questions about America and what we thought of Canadians, and I asked them a lot of the same questions back. It was late by the time I stumbled back to my van.

I hiked the Six Bridges Trail the next morning and into the early afternoon. The trail ended up being in the top ten hikes of the trip thus far. The path was not too difficult, but it was incredibly scenic. For the first mile or two, I encountered a lot of other people. After the point where most of them turned around, the trail thinned, and the scenery became even more grand. After the sixth bridge, the trail turned into a seldom used equestrian trail that I followed for a couple more miles until it looped back to the last bridge.

I got back to camp early and read for a few hours ,sitting in my hammock before the Canadians got back and invited me over for a fire and burgers. They said they got extra patties for me when they were in town.

I had been heavily rationing for the last couple weeks because I knew I was going to run out of money soon. Gas in Canada was more expensive than I thought it would be, and buying a tire would drain my account. Spending money on pot and booze hadn't helped my finances, but I felt like smoking and drinking here and there after long days of hiking satisfied a need. I wanted to make it out of Canada before I ran out of money, but to do that, I had to trim some budget fat. Groceries got cut. I hadn't bought groceries in almost two weeks, and I couldn't buy any more for the foreseeable future unless I made money somehow.

I was starting to feel actual hunger, so even thinking about a burger made my mouth water. We had a couple beers while we made the burgers and played some more cards. We shot the shit some more and got to know each other a little better. I told them I would be leaving the next morning, and they told me to come by for breakfast before I left. They had also bought extra bacon and eggs while they were in town.

In the morning, I dragged myself out of bed and made coffee for everyone while they cooked scrambled eggs, bacon, and toast. As we were cleaning up the picnic table, one of the Canadians dipped into the trailer and came out a minute later. He told me I was one of the good Americans. It had been fun to hang with me, he said, and they had a gift for me. From behind his back, he pulled out a camp knife and handed it to me. He said it was a pretty good knife from one of the most Canadian stores ever, Canadian Tire, and told me to use it and remember the beautiful parts of Canada.

With that, we all shook hands, and I climbed behind the wheel of the van, starting my journey South on The Icefields Parkway. The next big stop was Banff National Park.

The Icefields Parkway is the most beautiful drive in the world. It winds from Jasper National Park, through Banff, Yoho, and then down to Waterton Lakes National Parks. Around every bend of the road was a sight more beautiful than the last: several hundred-foot waterfalls on sheer cliffs; glacial lakes reflecting jagged snow-covered peaks; glaciers; dense forest; and bears. I could hardly imagine what beauty lay in the valley on the other side of the peaks.

I pulled into Lake Louise in the early evening and was shocked by the number of people. Many parking lots and busses ran from the lots to the lake. The lake is world-famous, but for some reason, I hadn't expected to encounter so many people. Jasper hadn't been nearly that busy. I hiked around the lake. The masses hadn't thinned even after a few miles, so

I turned back to my van to get away from all the bodies and cars. The atmosphere felt too much like an amusement park for my tastes.

I arrived at Moraine Lake an hour later and was happy to find it much less busy. One school bus full of people on a trip was in the sizeable parking lot, but Moraine was nowhere near as busy as Lake Louise. Moraine Lake is tucked back from the main highway. I walked around and took some photos. I was challenged trying to take a good photo of a lake with the 50mm lens. I wasn't happy with any of my shots, and nothing besides a photo of the canoes was worth keeping.

The sky was growing dark, so I decided to call it a night and sleep in the parking lot since I hadn't seen any quiet places to pull off during the last thirty minutes of driving. I was stoked to sleep so close to Moraine Lake, and I was planning to wake up at five to see the sun rise and the alpenglow light up the seven peaks surrounding the lake.

Five a.m. came, and I couldn't push myself out of bed for the sunrise. I was just so content in my warm bed, and it was so cold outside. I went back to sleep and woke up a couple hours later. Out of the back doors of the van, I made coffee and walked on the shore to look out at the lake. It was beautiful. I regretted not getting out of bed earlier, but I probably needed the sleep.

I bought some maple tea from the small gift shop and drove an hour on the highway to the town of Banff. I parked by the visitor's center, went in, then wandered around the city for a couple hours until it started raining and getting dark. I ducked into a mall to look at a map, hoping to find somewhere I could sleep since all the parking in the town was metered. A road by an airstrip looked promising for some pull-offs.

On the opposite side of the grass air strip, a small gravel lot was available for people to park in while climbing the Columbia Waterfall. I settled there for the night. From my windows, I had a view of the backside of Mt. Rundle, a grass field with a spectacular mountain backdrop, and the Columbia Waterfall peeking through the trees.

In the morning, I walked to the bottom of the waterfall, which was a lot farther away than I initially thought. The falls were much larger than they appeared from the parking lot.

I was a little tired, so I didn't want to do anything too strenuous that day. I spent a few hours driving around getting familiar with the area. At a picnic area, I set up my hammock and took a nap.

When the evening came, I went to the prettier places I had seen while looking for a pull-off and took a lot of photos. I was starting to get better with the 50mm. I was starting to learn how to position myself and frame the more beautiful or interesting parts of landscapes so I could make a landscape photo look complete and good without the photo being an all-inclusive, sweeping, wide angle shot.

I went back to the parking lot by the waterfall and shared it with someone traveling in a sprinter van.

I woke up early to go hike Mount Rundle. At the visitors' center I was told a few people had died on the hike, so I was stoked to try making it to the top. The trail wasn't marked well at all, and I ended up getting on the wrong path which crossed the river and went along the opposite side of Mount Rundle. The trail I meant to take was an all-day hike, so by the time I knew I had taken the wrong trail, it was too late to turn around and try to find the right one. I just enjoyed the leisurely trail I found myself on that followed a rushing river. I ate a granola bar at a small gazebo on the riverbank.

I had a lot of time left in the day after I finished the walk, so I went to the waterfall in the town of Banff, found a little park to hang at for a bit, then climbed Sulphur Mountain. On the way up, I made some hiking buddies who were on vacation from Calgary to hike and camp in the park. We joked around a lot and chatted about our lives. They told me I needed to go down to Waterton Lakes before going back to America. Waterton is connected to Glacier National Park in Montana. I was told Waterton had the same grandeur as Glacier but with way fewer tourists since it is a smaller park and on the Canadian side of the border. I had been told several times to go to Waterton, so I figured I had to go.

On the top of Sulphur Mountain was a viewing deck and the landing for a Gondola. The deck looked out over Banff far below and the beautiful Canadian Rockies that seemed to stretch on forever. Starting the trip, I had been most excited about going to the Pacific Northwest to see its nature, but the Canadian Rockies were filled with the most beautiful places I had ever been. For the most part, the Canadian Rockies are vast and unpopulated. Humanity has few marks there.

I spent another night in the same pull off by the air strip and spent a little time swiping on Tinder after the sun set. I matched with a couple women from Australia and New Zealand who were in Banff looking for a place to stay for the night since it was supposed to drop below freezing and they didn't have very warm sleeping bags. They had already found a place by the time we matched, but we made plans to split a campsite the next night.

I made coffee in the morning and skipped breakfast. My rationing was down to two granola bars per day and as much water as I could drink. I also tried to have something snacky like a handful of trail mix if I was driving around. I had finished all my canned soup about a week earlier, and only one box of granola bars remained. My plan was to eat one granola bar at the beginning of a hike and one for a late lunch or dinner until I ran out.

I had been feeling weaker, and I knew I was losing weight. The new hole punched in my belt told me that much. I hardly had any fat on me when I started the trip, and I had been hiking several miles every day. I couldn't have any fat on my bones now. I must be losing muscle mass. Getting on a scale would have scared me.

I continued up the road the airstrip was on. It ended at Two-Jack Lake. I spent most of the day swaying in a hammock looking out over the water before driving to the campground where I planned to meet the women I matched with on Tinder.

They had already set up the campsite when I pulled in. It was about dinner time, and they were making pasta for the three of us. I got out a bottle of wine for us to share. They were two of the most badass women I had ever met.

Zee was from New Zealand and was almost a doctor but had taken some time off to travel. She had been backpacking around the world for a few months and was in South America before coming up to Canada. She met Angie in South America. Zee got a job in Banff at the Ski resort and was going to stay there for the summer before going back home to New Zealand.

Angie was an engineer form Australia who got tired of the 9-5, had saved up some money, and decided to travel. She, too, had been backpacking the world for a couple months before she met Zee in South America, where they traveled together for about a month before finding out they had both booked flights on the same day to go up to Canada. From Canada, Angie was going to several countries in Europe and then to Asia before eventually wandering back to Australia. Her plan was to backpack the world for over a year, and she was more than halfway there by the time I met her.

Most women I've talked to are hesitant about traveling anywhere alone and would likely not do it, especially if they want to go to a different country or far-away state. But a few women are balls-to-the-wall and won't let anything stop them from traveling or doing what they want to do. I have an incredible amount of respect for these women. Women certainly face far more potential dangers traveling alone than men do. It is so incredibly unfortunate that we live in a world where half the population avoids solo adventures because of their sex, and I'm sickened to know that some people prey on women travelers.

We all packed up and left about the same time the next morning, and I got on the road south. I wanted to get a new tire before crossing the border because the dollar was in my favor in Canada. In the small town of Canmore, I dropped off my old, popped tire at a tire place and got a used, 80% tread tire much cheaper than a new tire. Eighty percent was good enough to be a spare.

While waiting on the tire work, I found a frisbee golf course at the Nordic Ski Center up in the mountains. The course followed the ski track and wove through the forest. After the round of disc golf, I walked around the center until I got a call from the tire shop.

With a new spare and an almost empty bank account, I got back on the highway for several hours of driving to Waterton Lakes. I stopped at a Canadian Tire to sleep for the night about an hour north of the park.

Wind gusted hard through the night and continued into the day. The air was bitingly cold when I got to Waterton, too cold and windy for any good hiking. I was feeling even weaker, so I knew I wouldn't be up for a long hike anyway. Instead, I parked by Waterton Lake where I had a nice view of the massive hilltop chalet. I ate an edible I had been saving. I got out to take some photos, but for the most part, I napped and watched movies on my laptop.

When evening came, the wind had died down, and I had sobered up, so I drove to Red Rock Canyon. One of the things Glacier and Waterton National Parks are known for is the multicolored rocks. The amount of iron present determines the color of the rocks. Most of the rocks are shades of green or red. In the case of Red Rock Canyon, well, it is pretty much what the name describes. It is a small canyon with vibrant red rock with white veins and a small stream of glacial blue water flowing at the bottom.

On one of the red outcroppings just above the small creek, a couple people were setting up what looked like a fancy picnic. It looked interesting, and I guessed at what was coming later.

I went farther down the path and saw a trail sign to a waterfall about a half mile away. I arrived at the falls in a few minutes. Like every other place I had seen in Waterton and the Canadian Rockies, the waterfall and view up at the towering mountains was breathtaking.

The sky started to turn pink, and I hurried back to the canyon. A small footbridge ran over the canyon forty feet downstream from where the picnic was set up. A few smiling people were standing on the bridge looking at the canyon and at the well-dressed couple who now faced each other as they ate and drank on the red rock ledge. We all knew what was going to happen.

When the colors in the sky were at their peak of vibrance for the evening, the man got on one knee beside the table. We couldn't hear her response, but we knew she said yes. Everyone on the bridge cheered them on. It was such a beautiful thing to witness, and it gave me some ideas for a proposal of my own one day.

I spent my last night in Canada in the parking lot by Red Rock Canyon. My Canadian stint was over. I was off to America the next day. I went to bed hungry but happy.

Canada had treated me well. I saw some of the most beautiful places that the Western provinces had to offer. I didn't want to leave. I wanted to turn around and go back to the Icefields Parkway, return to Banff or Jasper, but I knew it was time to start the last leg of my journey.

For the whole trip, I had made a point of not paying attention to time, schedules, or calendar dates. When time wasn't confined to a page of numbered boxes, I felt more connected to the earth around me. I went places and did things when the time felt right. Often, I had no clue what the day was. Time lost some of its meaning, and I was happier for it. I felt some sadness when leaving new or enthralling places and people, but I knew that something exciting would always be on the horizon.

Throughout my life, I feel like I have been walking down a long corridor with many doors on both sides. As I walk alone down the hall, I open most of the doors. I just peek into some. I step fully through others. I don't close doors behind me. Each door is a different path my life could go, a different opportunity or person or place. After some time behind a door, I return to the corridor and keep walking. I keep going in and coming out because I'm curious about what's behind the doors I have not yet opened. Curiosity makes me stir-crazy and itching to leave even the most comfortable of settings. Sometimes I look back at all those still-open doors that lead to so many different places and people, and I wonder if I have opened too many.

14. Glacier

Toughen up. Life is not easy. Life is not clean. Life is hard and messy. Life is suffering. Our species consisted of hunter and gatherer nomads not so long ago. Those who were injured were injured or couldn't keep up were left to die. Our day to day lives are much easier now, thousands of years later, but the struggle to survive continues. Whatever difficulty is in front of you right now, it is not so bad, just a little challenge. The hardest days and the darkest nights are always yet to come, and if you want to have any hope of surviving it or of being able to hold your chin up on the other side, toughen up and shoulder through whatever is in front of you now. You will make it through.

At whatever point in our lives we face our greatest challenge, it is better to have already gone through many other challenges and hardships, so the greatest challenge does not seem overwhelming or impossible, just difficult. If we spend our lives avoiding difficulty and hardship, then surely when retreat is not an option in the face of a challenge of any size, we could be crushed.

When you consider a knife, one of the most crucial elements is the temper of the steel. Temper is unseeable. It is a physical property that has no physical appearance. Temper can be measured only by special files or by specialized technology.

If the blade is too hard, it will break before it bends. It will be harder to sharpen but will keep its edge for a longer time. It can take abuse, but when you strike with it or pry with it in just the wrong way, the blade could snap, ruining the knife. There is no saving it. The knife will be worthless.

If the steel is too soft, the blade will require constant sharpening, and in the face of any abuse, it will bend out of shape. The edge will fold and roll. Attempting to bend the blade back and put a new edge on it is an endless process because it will suffer the same fate ad infinitum. If the steel is too hard or too soft, the knife isn't good for much more than gentle use or display. But a knife is a working tool, and life is seldom gentle.

The good knife is strong and tough. It is between hard and soft. It can be sharpened in the field without much difficultly. It holds an edge well, but it does not bend easily. Only at its limit, the blade bends. It does not break. The knife can be fixed with the proper tools and in the proper hands. The good knife is the knife that your grandfather passes down. Though the sheath, handle, and blade may be beat to hell over the decades, the steel will still be good.

Glacier National Park was a test of my temper. It was a challenge designed to find my limit and test if I would bend or break. Maybe the whole trip had been a test. I was alone. I was a thousand miles from home. I had no money, and I was starving. Good God was I hungry. I could count all my ribs. I was a dirty, drunk teenager crying into can of green beans on a Tuesday afternoon after cutting a hike short because my body had reached its limits. After I cried into the burnt can of beans, I realized I had not broken; I had bent.

But for me to bend, my ego had to break. I had to give up the stance that I was doing everything by myself. I had to give up on the idea that I was somehow above anyone else.

Heading into Glacier, I had found myself looking at a piece of cardboard in the van, wondering what I should write on it so people might want to give me a couple dollars as I stood on the shoulder of the road. I had to trade my pride for hopes of mercy.

There was not much more I could physically do in Glacier, but I had this campsite for another full day. After cutting the Lincoln Lake hike short, I didn't want to attempt more hikes. I knew if I tried, I would again risk passing out. I didn't need to learn the same lesson a second time.

After I'd eaten the beans, sobered, up and dried the tears from my cheeks, I felt better.

Not being hungry was an amazing feeling, and I decided to celebrate by walking the short distance to the edge of the lake. I spent some time on the shore of Lake McDonald.

I stood up to my knees and waded around in the crystal-clear water, and I skipped green and red colored rocks across its smooth surface. The mountain peaks shrouded in low hanging clouds reminded me of just how small everything really is.

How many days had these mountains seen? How many people and trees and glaciers had these mountains seen come and go?

It dawned on me that asking for help didn't mean I failed. Everyone needs help at some point, and I had been helped countless times in the last four months whether I knew it at the time or not. Because of loving family and kind strangers, I had done so much more than I otherwise could have.

It's odd how at peace we feel when we are reminded how small and insignificant we are. I think feeling small and insignificant is the opposite of what we usually want to feel, but it is what we need to feel. Otherwise, we bear the imagined burden of carrying and continuing our species individually.

Millions of people want to feel important and deserving of something more. But this life, these desires bring agony, stress, turmoil, and drama. Ego is a lie, and internally, we know it. Of the billions of people who have walked this earth, maybe only be a couple hundred make enough difference to be remembered for their efforts. Even CEOs and presidents of multinational corporations will never be remembered like Plato, or Einstein, or Newton, or Picasso are. Most of us will be forgotten, and that's okay.

Tormenting the soul as we do, believing we are more important than we are is great agony. Holding imagined weight of importance, we are caged animals who have built our own locks. We are not free; we cannot achieve peace and freedom until we overcome our ego.

We can leave our cage whenever we choose. The bars of self-expectations dissipate when we free ourselves from the desire to be important.

The stars teach us. They remind us of our size, and we are better for it. When we recognize our smallness, we can forgive ourselves our shortcomings. When we realize we lose our lives rushing towards our future, we can learn patience and acceptance in the here and now.

Whether or not we will be remembered by future generations, in the now we are still creators and spreaders of culture, ideas, new creations, and new technology. We are capable of and should strive toward being the greatest version of ourselves, and we should learn as much as possible to contribute the most to our own lives and to the betterment of the world around us.

I thought about these things sitting by my campfire my last night in Glacier, smoking a joint and sipping on a beer. I had come to what was supposed to happen. Tomorrow I would leave the park and embark on the home stretch of the journey.

When I first left home, I had a goal to travel 10,000 miles and be gone for five months. Though I wouldn't reach the five months, I had already exceeded the distance. At Glacier, I had traveled just shy of 12,000 miles and still had lots of driving left to do before getting back to Missouri. Plus, I didn't have to go home immediately. I could still stretch the trip a couple weeks by staying with family and friends.

Looking back at everything I had been through, the adventures, the people, the sites . . . I learned so much. And I realized I still had much to learn. I was a young man discovering how to navigate my life in a big, changing world. Of course, the trip didn't go how I wanted it to go; I wouldn't have learned anything if it had. I was where I needed to be, not where I wanted to be.

I was down for the first part of Glacier, but I was comparing myself to where I was before I got my injury. A little more than a year ago, I could barely do anything for myself and needed a lot of medical treatments. I could barely remember my name. Since then, I had worked full time jobs. I had traveled around many states and Canadian provinces. I had become a better photographer, and I had gone more than a month without a spinal adjustment. What blessings, to be able to do all that only a short time after a life altering injury.

Looking at my life over the course of a year rather than over the course of a week created a massive shift in my thinking. Instead of being frustrated with myself for being hungry and broke far from home, I became thankful for my growth and for the people who helped me along the way.

Even with the pain of hunger, I would do it all again without batting an eye. It had been one hell of an adventure, and it wasn't finished yet. I would still be able to make it through Yellowstone, Wyoming, and South Dakota before getting back to Missouri. More adventure lay ahead of me. After all, I was in Glacier National Park, one of the coolest places in the world.

Remembering I had seen a bike trail not too far away, I pulled my longboard out from the back of the van. I needed to move and wanted to see where the trail went. I took a swig of gin and tossed the board onto the road.

I pushed for miles, and the path took me alongside rivers and through tall coniferous trees. The more I pushed and the harder the wind hit my face, the happier I was. Everything was going to be okay, even if it was not ideal. Life does not give us everything we want or what we deserve. It gives us what we need, and that is a real miracle.

Through several months and over many mountains, I thought I was in it alone, but I wasn't. with almost every big challenge I faced, someone else was there. Whether I was with a stranger in a Zion campground, a welcoming group of people at Lake Powell, or a lover in Oregon, I was never fully alone. Even during the days when I didn't see another soul, I wasn't really by myself. How could I be alone when I was little more than a messy combination of all the people in my life with my own crazy little twist added in?

Growing up, I thought that once I became a man, I would be finished growing. I would be an adult and ready to face the world with whatever tools I had. I thought I had to be ready to do everything by myself. At the time I thought manhood meant I would be a more independent and even stronger person who others could rely on. I thought most of my growing would be behind me and I would have confidence in my sense of self. I thought I was no longer going to ask for or need help but, instead, would be the one helping others. Those were still the thoughts of a boy.

Becoming a man is the opposite of all of that. Manhood is a recognition that the easy part is over. Challenges never cease to confront us and threaten our sense of self. Becoming a man means learning that it is foolish to think anyone can go through life alone. Becoming a man, to me, means letting pride go, taking a deep breath, and asking for help.

The last morning in the campsite, I knew it was time to leave Glacier and Montana. I felt I had done what I needed to do there. The time had come to leave this room, go back into the corridor, and find a new door to open and explore.

15. Coming Down from the High

As I left Glacier, I called up a few high school friends who worked in Yellowstone. I asked if they would be free to go on a hike or show me around the park for a day and if they knew any places I could park and sleep for free in the park. All the campgrounds inside of and surrounding the park had been booked up for months. They said I could stay in an empty room in one of the employee bunkhouses in Canyon Village that was reserved for visiting friends and family. It would only be a few bucks per night, and I would also get a discount on food at a couple of the restaurants in the village. How could I say no?

The entrance at West Yellowstone was a bombardment of tourist shops, restaurants, and No Vacancy signs lit up in front of motels. Along the road were more signs for campgrounds, also without vacancy. I had totally forgotten people often booked these places out months in advance since Yellowstone is such a beautiful and popular place.

I made it to the gate, showed my national parks pass, and then I was in. A massive, otherworldly place full of steam vents, multicolored bacterial growths in hot springs, boiling mud pots, geysers, bears, bison, and wolves awaited me. I could smell the awaiting adventures; they smelled like sulfur.

I had been to Yellowstone with family on one of our summer road trips several years earlier. I remembered a few things like the visitor's center, The Grand Canyon of Yellowstone, Old Faithful, Mammoth Hot Springs, and Yellowstone Lake, but all those memories were blurry. My friends didn't get off work until the evening. It was barely noon now, so I had plenty of time to kill before I was going to meet them in Canyon Village.

A few miles into the park, I stopped at a picnic area right on the Yellowstone River and got out of my van to sit in the sun and write. Downstream stood a pair of fly fishers standing up to their thighs in the water. On the other side of the meadow sat a handful of grazing bison. Aside from the noise of cars that occasionally passed by, it was pure heaven.

The first thing I wanted to see was Old Faithful. I wanted to see that first because I knew the area would be filed with people. I hoped to get that out of the way first and then try to find the less busy parts of the park. I suppose almost everyone's goal in a National Park is to be surrounded by nature instead of people and cars.

At Old Faithful, I parked minutes after the most recent eruption, so I would have to wait about an hour and a half before the next. Ninety minutes was plenty of time to walk around on the boardwalks that zig zagged their way through the valley and around small geysers, steam vents, and mud pots. A half mile onto the trail, I saw a lone wolf come out of the tree line and walk to the boardwalk a hundred feet in front of me. He jumped on it, stopped, looked around, then walked fifty feet on the path before jumping off and prancing back into the trees.

That was my first time seeing a wolf not trapped in a glass cage at a zoo. This wolf seemed attentive but relaxed, like it was totally accustomed to skirting around bubbling mud and hopping on the boardwalk because he belonged there. He did not seem to care about people in the slightest. Wolves at the zoo always looked forlorn with eyes, ears, and tail down, lacking the glint of the wild in their eyes. This wolf looked perfectly at home, at ease, strong, and proud.

After seeing this wolf and other animals I had come across in the last few months, I had grown a distaste for zoos. They are a mark of separation from nature, an attempt to humanize the animals and make the wild docile. We put animals that need miles to roam inside small cages, prisons, for their entire lives. We soften their survival skills, and when they try to defend themselves from their captors, they are punished even more (RIP Harambe). We make them into a sad spectacle for people to see on the weekends or their day off. We do to animals what we have done to ourselves. Survival is no longer dependent on our pack or our skillset, but on sitting in one place doing tricks and biding time, waiting for food to be tossed our way. The beauty of an animal is not their pelts or in what parlor tricks they can do, the same way the beauty of a person is not in the clothing they wear or the paint on their faces. The beauty of an animal lies in their wild spirit that challenges the command to be tame.

Oh, but it's for their own good, we say! They don't have to worry about predators in zoos, and they live longer than they would if they were in the wild. Surely, they appreciate the trade of freedom for security, right? I wonder if that idea is entirely human. I have never seen a wolf as contented, proud, and healthy looking as the wild wolf I saw on the boardwalk. Its life was much better in the wild than it would have been in any zoo, even if it wasn't tossed food at regular intervals. I knew that just from the way the wolf carried itself in the few seconds I saw it. I knew that because I have felt the freedom the wolf had, and I wouldn't trade that freedom for any amount of comfort or security.

When the wolf dipped back into the trees, I was taken out of my trance, and I kept on walking and taking photos of some of the geysers. I passed a couple older women on the boardwalk, and I overheard them complaining about how the park didn't have good cell service and how, for the next family trip, they wouldn't go somewhere as far away from civilization.

That upset me. Here was one of the most beautiful and geologically interesting places in all North America. There were geysers, waterfalls, bears, bison, rivers, mountains, and sprawling forest. On top of that, a good chunk of Yellowstone is situated inside one of the largest volcano calderas in North America. How cool is that? The area is abundant in life and splendor, and this person was bitching about not being able to check her Facebook. I started to really understand the distress of that old man in Canyonlands.

Back at the employee bunkhouse, I met up with Kailey, and we went for a walk to the Grand Canyon on the Yellowstone. We walked, talked, and caught up. We hadn't seen each other in the year since we graduated high school.

We went first to Lower Falls, then walked on the road to Upper Falls.

When we got back from the walk, we had enough time to eat dinner before some other employees told us to pack a bag to go to Little Canyon. We grabbed hiking packs, a few beers, a little liquor, and our pot. We wandered miles into the woods on a horse trail before leaving the trail until we came to a steeply slanted cliff that we climbed down. Less than ten feet below the top of the cliff, we came upon a small cave big enough to fit five out of the seven of us. We hotboxed the cave, and when the joint was cashed, we finished the climb down to the bottom of the little canyon and followed the creek until we saw a fire pit and a cow skull hung on a tree. We all set up hammocks in the surrounding trees while someone lit a fire in the rock circle next to the creek.

Drinks and joints were passed, and the flames licked the sky until the blue of the day faded into black. Crossfaded and stuffing our hammocks back into their stuff sacks, we realized no one brought flashlights because we hadn't planned on being out that late. Our intoxicated group was in the middle of bear country in the dark woods of Yellowstone in a place off the trail that only three of the people in that group had been to before. Two people pulled out phone flashlights. The others had either left phones behind or their phones were dead.

We made our way out of the canyon, through the woods until we found the trail that we followed through a field to a road, and eventually back to the bunkhouse. By the end of the hike, we were being led by only one iPhone flashlight and the light of the full moon poking through the canopy. With a group that big, we didn't have to worry much about bears. We chatted loudly the whole walk back so the bears didn't bother us. We got back at two in the morning, and I passed out hard.

I woke up late and made coffee in the back of my van in the parking lot down the hill. After coffee and a light breakfast, a few of us went off to smoke pot in the woods. I had no plans for the day besides maybe going on a walk to see the Grand Canyon again, so coffee and a joint was the perfect way to start the day. After that, my friends went off to work. I walked back up to the bunkhouses to see what sort of trouble I could get into. This was probably going to be the last unpredictable part of the road trip, and I wanted to live it up.

In places like this without a strong connection to Wi-Fi or cell service, plans are made the old-fashioned way: bumping into people, talking, and planning for later that day. Several hammocks were set up in the trees between the bunkhouses, and people with the day off or on break usually chilled there. While I was wandering around looking for familiar faces, someone I had briefly met when I first arrived found me and invited me to watch the sun set from the top of Mount Washburn with a group of staff that night. So that took care of the nightly adventure, but I still needed to fill the rest of the day.

I hopped in the van and headed west from Canyon Village. I really wanted to see Obsidian Cliff. When I turned north, I encountered road construction. The road to Obsidian Cliff was closed. That was a little disappointing, but oh well, there was still plenty of cool stuff to see.

In another forty-five minutes I made it to Mammoth Hot Springs and struggled to find a place to park. This area was even busier than the west entrance and around Canyon Village. I wasn't ready for that. In places, cars lined the road. Mostly older people had set up lawn chairs in the grass to look at meadows, mountainous views, and herds of bison that grazed and napped in the warm afternoon sun.

I pulled into the parking lot for Mammoth Hot Springs and had to drive through the loop four times before a parking spot opened up. National Parks can be kind of a Catch 22. You go there to get away from society and cities to see the beauty of the natural world, and so does everyone else. Popular places are popular for a reason, though, so even the packed places in Yellowstone are still worth seeing.

I wandered around the trails after I parked and took a lot of photos. I wanted to sit and look at a few of the hot springs and colorful bacteria growths for a while, but there were so many people walking by I would have felt too in the way. I slowly made my way back to the van and was passed by dozens of people barely pausing to take photos of the formations. I didn't have cell service, and I had left the park map on my bed back in the bunkhouse. I left the parking lot and just started driving.

Slowly making my way around the northern loop of the park, I stopped often along the side of the road to take photos of the views or to read informational signs. After a few hours, I ended up back at Canyon Village. I decided to take it easy the rest of the day and edit some photos I had taken in Glacier and Yellowstone. I was still exhausted from the late-night excursions, so I took a nap before the Mt. Washburn trip.

Just before golden hour, I found the guy who invited me to watch the sunset and stargaze. He, along with ten other people, were packing up a truck and a jeep with blankets and booze. I was wearing several layers and had a warm hat on. It was going to be cold at 10,000 feet at night.

There were eleven of us in total, and we only had the two vehicles. The truck only had one bench seat that could fit three, and the jeep had five seats. So naturally, I volunteered to be one of the three people to ride in the bed of the truck, covered up by a tarp. I had no idea how long the drive would take, but I was one of the people dressed the warmest. Riding up a mountain in a truck bed sounded like fun

The drive ended up being about forty minutes, and it was frigid even with the tarp and several layers. Those of us under the tarp tried talking and passing the flask around to warm up, but that didn't work too well. After we started feeling switchbacks, we figured it was safe enough to sit up. We pulled the tarp off our top halves and saw the golden sun just starting to dip behind the peaks and turn the few clouds bright pink.

We unpacked in the parking lot at the top of a ridge near the peak of Mount Washburn. One side of the ridge faced west to the sunset, and the other faced east at the darkening sky. We stood with our faces in the wind and passed bottles around. The sky turned from blue to yellow to gold to orange.

When we couldn't stand the wind anymore and the color had all but faded, we migrated the fifty feet to the other side of the ridge and walked downhill a little bit to get out of the wind.

As the light disappeared, and as we got drunker, the stars started to come out like I had never seen them. Until then, the best stars I had seen were in Bryce Canyon. The stars there were incredible but still came short of the stars from Mount Washburn. The Milky Way appeared over the peak in vibrant colors. We could see all the clouds in the galaxy peppered by the occasional shooting star. Two of us had brought cameras to try to capture the stars; we got out our cameras and tripods and set them up on the steep slope.

I had tried astrophotography a couple times before and had gotten a couple good shots from Bryce, but overall, I wasn't too confident with my skills. Most of what I did with the camera was still guess work. Especially being drunk and limited to a 50mm lens, getting the shots I had in my head wasn't easy. A lot of the photos had star smears, or the whole photo was blurry. Only a couple ended up looking cool.

Sometime after two a.m., we decided to head back. The drivers had stayed mostly sober, and we all piled back into the vehicles. The bed of the pickup was even colder than it had been, but we were warmer because we were drunk. For the first part of the drive, we sat up in the bed to continue watching the stars as we drove through the quiet mountain scape.

My last hurrah was the perfect way to come down from the high I had been riding since I left home. It was simple, really. Watching the sunset and stars come out was really nothing too special; I had done it dozens, maybe hundreds of times before. It's something that happens every single night everywhere in the world. But tonight, I was experiencing it with new and old friends, making questionable decisions on top of a mountain, which was good closure for the past few months. Drunk, sitting in the bed of a pickup truck driving down a mountain half covered by a tarp at 2:30 in the morning, I felt content. As much as I knew I would hate myself the next couple days for multiple nights of heavy drinking in a row, it was worth it. No good story ever started with, "One time I went to bed early."

The next day, I left the park and drove over the Fisherman's Bridge and up the mountains to the East Entrance of the park. I was planning on making a beeline through Wyoming to Sheridan to see Cousin Isiah, but I hadn't called him yet to let him know I was coming. I hadn't had service in Yellowstone, so once I got to Cody, I pulled over and called him up. He was hosting a family reunion with the other side of his family and had a packed house. He assured me that I was more than welcome, but he was really concerned about where I would sleep. All the beds, couches, and most of the floors were already occupied. He didn't know where to put me. I had to stop him from talking because I could tell it was stressing him. I laughed and told him it was no problem at all, that I had been sleeping in a van for the last few months. I was bringing a bed to sleep on. I told him if he had a place for me to park, I would be comfortable. He breathed a big sigh of relief.

Several hours of driving through the open land of Wyoming laid between me and Isiah's ranch. Wyoming was one of the states I was largely unfamiliar with, and I had thought of it as empty. I was right. It was empty of people. The land is beautiful. Driving from Yellowstone to Sheridan gave me an appreciation for the state that I had not had before. There was so much open space and seemingly untouched land.

When I pulled up to the ranch house, I was greeted with hugs by Isiah and Ruth, their dogs, and about twenty other removed family members who I didn't know. The first thing they did was offer to feed me, and I could have cried. As with most family gatherings, food was abundant, and everything was homemade. After barely eating anything for so long, I couldn't eat much before getting stomach cramps. Even with the cramps, Being full felt amazing.

Upon learning that I was a full four months into a Western America and Western Canada road trip, the family had a lot of questions about how things had been going, what things I had done, and how much I was eating. When I told them about the last part, they immediately offered me more food and continued doing so at least once an hour. I hadn't been sure how crashing a family reunion would go, but I after I got there, I never felt like I was crashing anything. Very soon after I pulled up, they made me feel like part of their family. Everyone welcomed me.

Time passed slowly at the ranch. Days were full of board games, cooking, shooting prairie dogs, exploring the ranch on four-wheelers, and writing. Each night I sat at the kitchen table, well into the night, writing a much lengthier and final blog post. I had been bad about keeping up with the online blog since I had gotten into Canada, and I had done much living to catch up in writing with since then. I was eager to finish up the blog and be done with it, to move onto something new. The non-edited, journal style entries had gotten harder to force myself to write, especially as I got better at photography. I just wanted to post photos, but I had started with a blog and writing so that's how I would finish, too.

Family started trickling away a couple days after I arrived; I had come towards the end of the reunion. One of the days, a van load of the family wanted to go to Yellowstone. I had just made that drive and didn't really want to go back for a drive around the Yellowstone loop. I wanted to explore the ranch some more. I left on a four-wheeler when the others left in their van, and I spent a lot of time meandering up and down hills and sitting by the river that divided Wyoming from Montana.

It was quiet. And the quiet was deafening. The roar of silence in nature is hidden at first, and it takes practice to hear it. The silence can be a bird's wings buffeting the wind or pine needles rustling in the breeze. A treasure of sound can be heard in man's silence. When man is muted and society crumbles away to the far end of the horizon, when everything manufactured is stripped away, the self can be found. When we rush around trying to impress or please everyone, our selves are lost.

My generation and certainly the one before mine are afraid of finding ourselves. Our friends and possessions become security blankets and brands we throw out to the world hoping for recognition and approval. But our groups and things are not the way to happiness, peace, or knowledge of the self. We are too concerned with making something to cover our insecurities to realize we have nothing at all to be insecure about. By displaying ourselves how we wish to be seen and by lying to ourselves about who we are, we can grow ancient and still be ignorant children playing silly games. Finding ourselves is a similar process to finding silence in nature. It requires escape, purpose, contemplation, a shift in perception and above all, openness. We find ourselves, not by creating an image of ourselves to show the world, but by being naked and letting ourselves find us.

What the road trip had really given me was my first opportunity to be selfish and to find out what I wanted in life far away from societal pressures. At home, I had all sorts of responsibilities and obligations. What I did often depended quite a bit on someone else. For the past four months, I had done what I wanted when I wanted to do it. If I wanted to hike to a waterfall, I did it. If I wanted to be lazy and get high or drunk, I got a campsite and had a great time. If I wanted to talk to someone, I made friends. If I wanted to challenge myself creatively, I took photos, wrote, or read. I had been open to opportunities, people, and experiences. After knowing what it was like to lose my identity, the trip was a chance to start a journey to find me, starting with a blank slate. Far away from anyone who knew me well and in unfamiliar lands, I could learn who I was with no fetter of societal standards or obligations.

The days kept passing at Isiah's, and the family reunion party dwindled. We went on a family picnic in the Bighorns, spent more time tooling around the ranch, playing games, and telling stories. I spent a clear night trying astrophotography from Isiah's driveway, and the photos turned out better than they had at Yellowstone, probably because I was sober.

I felt so much healthier at Isiah's than I had in the last month or so. Everyone was consistently making sure I was fed, and my ribs were starting to hide in my chest. Isiah's place was the longest I had stayed in one place since Martin's in San Diego, and the short reprieve from my transiency was welcome. After enough of the family had gone, Isiah and Ruth were quick to pull me inside to sleep on a real bed, and it was nice. I felt like I was staying in a hotel. But after a couple days, I started to miss my van bed the way I missed my home bed during long vacations as a kid.

I was the last to leave Isiah's. I had been there more than a week, but they wanted me to stay longer. They didn't get visitors up there much, and it was hard for them to get away and travel to see family with so much land to take care of. I wanted to stay another couple months. Maybe I should have stayed. I could have helped a lot on the ranch. Isiah and Ruth would have enjoyed having me there.

But I knew it was time to pull the band-aid off. The trip was over. It was time to leave and make my last stop before going back to the place I had begun my journey.

16. Fireworks

My initial, tentative plan after Glacier was to go through the Midwest until I hit Lake Superior, then follow it up to where I would meet my dad at Isle Royal, the smallest of the national parks. We would backpack the length of the island for a couple days before going back to the mainland. After Isle Royal, I would cross the Canadian border again and be in Thunder Bay in time to celebrate Canada Day. I had never seen how another country celebrated their independence, but I wanted to have the experience. Toronto and Quebec would be next. Then I would drop back into the U.S. through Michigan's upper peninsula, follow Lake Michigan down to Illinois to see a lot of family, and finally return to Missouri two weeks before I was supposed to move into the dorms at Millikin in Illinois.

After passing through the Badlands, I wanted so badly to turn off cruise control and take the next exit that would put me on a road going north. I now had a few hundred dollars from my parents in my bank account. That would pay for gas and the necessities for food to make it through Canada. Then I would be with family after getting to Illinois, and they would feed me. So, I really would only need to pay for about two weeks of minimal food and a couple hundred miles worth of gas. I could do it. It would just be one more month on the road. I knew this would be the last time I would be able to go on a trip like this for a long time, and I wanted to squeeze every drop of it.

College wasn't necessarily something I wanted to do. A life of wanderlust fueled gallivanting around the world with no career or checked boxes on my resume sounded so much more fulfilling than a diploma and being pushed into a career. I would be content being little more than a wanderer for my whole life. The four months I had just spent on the road had only confirmed that desire. I was scared of the thought of going to some higher education institution where I would have to follow the rules of bureaucratic overlords and starve my spirit in order to get a degree I would never use except as a line on my resume. Living in Illinois, far away from the mountains and clean lakes and rivers, was utterly unappealing and sounded depressing.

I had spent months waking up and looking outside my window to the most picturesque mountain and lake views I had ever seen in my life. I spent the days wandering through ancient forests, up mountains, and down into deep canyons. Soon, I would have to trade that lifestyle for four years of living in brick buildings at a place where the smell of soy and pollution hung in the air thick enough to taste. I knew the transition would be one of the more difficult things I had done even though I was a little excited about experiencing something new. Four years of putting my life on hold to receive a piece of paper that said I was trained for a job put a bad taste in my mouth.

Alas, I was resigned to the decisions I had made when I wasn't tapping my foot by the gas pedal of my home on wheels. I steered through the Badlands and Black Hills of South Dakota without even stopping to take a photo. I turned off the road only for gas until I pulled against the curb by the South Dakota Bergland's home in the small town of Beresford.

It was nice, though a little weird, to see familiar faces again, people I wouldn't have to introduce myself to. In the four months I was gone, I had maybe spent a total of three weeks with people I knew. Everyone else was a stranger, someone I didn't know well, or someone I hadn't seen in years.

My South Dakota family welcomed me with hugs. I took my backpack inside. It felt a little odd to be invited in where a room with a bed was ready for me while my home was parked outside the window. I would have been just as content sleeping in the driveway.

I spent a few days with the South Dakota Berglands. I went to the town pool, went shooting with my uncle, and hung out with my cousins and aunt when they were home.

For a few evenings, I went to my cousin's friend's house to sit around a fire with some drinks.

I had originally planned on being in Thunder Bay, Ontario for Canada Day, then staying in Canada through the Fourth of July. But as life would have it, I was in Beresford, South Dakota, for both.

On the Fourth, my cousin took me out to a back road away from town where a lot of people he knew had gathered for fireworks. There were no real plans for the night other than to play around with fireworks and drink beer. It was a chill evening until someone pulled out artillery shells. Other people there knew what was going on when the guy put the tube on the ground and angled it 45 degrees in the middle of the road. I was just along for the ride when people started lining up as if we were about to race. Turns out, that's kind of what we were doing.

The game was to start running down the road as the artillery shell was lit so that it would explode not too far above our heads and potentially but hopefully not hit one of us. We did this a handful of times, and surprisingly, no one got burned. Before midnight, everyone had packed up in their cars and driven back into town.

Before I left South Dakota, I finished up my last blog post from the road that spanned from Alberta to South Dakota. With this last post, I wanted to make the text longer, more in depth, and more honest. For the most part, it was about the same as other posts, but I tried to be a little more honest and reflective about who I was in South Dakota compared to who I was when I left home. I had come a long way. Before leaving, I was an expert at swallowing my emotions to be neutral, to get by easily and be unaffected by things.

As I had been told by several strangers on the road, feelings demand to be felt. Swallowing emotions is not dealing with them. Feelings need to be let out. They need to be felt if there is to be any hope of moving on from the past and growing into who we are supposed to be. Holding emotions in is clinging to the past, and the past is already gone. Maybe it never even existed at all. There is only now, and to genuinely live, one must live in today and let go of yesterday. Unfortunately, I don't think I was a good enough writer at the time to express any of this as clearly as I wanted to.

I had spent the last days in South Dakota with my family picking wild asparagus, going to the range, lounging, and just hanging out. Then the time came for me to go. I knew I was in the last little bit of the story. Though I didn't want it to end, I knew it had to. It is best to allow the story to end at the right time as opposed to holding on too tight and forcing something to happen that wasn't meant to be. In my bones, unconsciously, I knew it was time to make the four-hour trek down I-29 and color in the last short line on my tattered atlas to complete the circuit. I hugged my aunt, uncle, and cousins, thanking them, and climbed in the van.

The last hour and a half of the drive was the same as the first hour and a half of the drive several months earlier. Again, I was confronted by the feeling of familiarity. I wasn't sure what to do with that feeling after months of unfamiliar being the norm. So, I did about the only thing I could think to do; I turned on "Let's Go" by Matt and Kim, shouted the lyrics, and pounded on the steering wheel as the Shaggin' Wagon barreled down the hot asphalt.

17. I Found My Name

I lost my name when I hit my head. I can't tell you exactly how it feels to have the most foundational thing to your identity slip between your fingers like burning hot sand, but it is similar to being absolutely lost in your hometown after years of being away. Everything has a sense of familiarity to it, but you have no clue where exactly you are.

I learned the necessity and meaninglessness of having a name. A name is who I was, and everything I did was banked around it. It was the central point from which everything I did stretched out. You see, I had plans. I was becoming established in a lifestyle. I was getting a foothold in entrepreneurship. I had a plan in place for my college years, and I had an idea of what I wanted to do and where I wanted to be after that. In a moment, all that got flipped on its head, and suddenly, there was no central point anywhere. I was no longer my name. I was just a tangled mess of broken thoughts and stabbing headaches. But even without a name, life doesn't stop. The sun still rose and set. The wind still blew whether I had a name or not.

After I recovered from my diving injury and started to get back on track of going through the motions of a semblance of what my life was, I wasn't magically cured. I still remembered being lost in the familiar. I could remember my name, but my life felt like pants that didn't fit anymore.

When people asked why I was going to live in a van, I told them it was because I wanted to see the world or because I wanted to challenge myself or because I was so tired from everything that had happened, and I just needed to get away. While that was all true, the entire reason encompassed much more. As cliché as it sounds, I left on my rubber tramp version of "Into the Wild" because I needed to find myself. If I was lost in the familiar, maybe I could find my way in the unfamiliar.

I saw and did a lot of once-in-a-lifetime sorts of things on the road. I got lost many times. I thought I was alone most of the time, but that wasn't true. I just had to look in a mirror with a dirty face and see into the eyes of strangers to understand that I wasn't alone. I thought I was looking for myself, but I had been there the whole time with my identity intact.

I befriended people everywhere I went. I got into strangers' cars on a whim, picked up hitch hikers, and camped with strangers not because I got some perverted adrenaline rush from potential danger; in fact, the opposite was true. Not once did I feel that rush with new people or scenarios. I approached every person with the belief that no matter who we are, where we come from, or what we look like, we have something in common, and we can build from whatever commonality that is.

We are white, we are black, we are Christian, we are Muslim, we are atheists, we are socialists, we are republicans, we are communists, we are vegans, we are hunters, we are farmers, we are bankers, we are old, we are young. We give ourselves titles and too often use these titles as fillers for our names and identities. Too often, we define ourselves as being this and not that because identifying with a group is for some reason easier than identifying as a human like every other human just trying to live a good, happy life and to get by in this fucked up, beautiful world. Our titles are just descriptions of a small part of our lives. Even when our titles conflict with other people, we all still have more commonalities than differences.

I found who I am. I put a name to my identity, and more than that, I can now describe who I am. I am little more than a combination of everyone I have ever met with a little bit of my own style and personality acting as the glue. Humanity is a cosmic spider web, and we are all flies caught on interconnected strands, destined to be stuck together and in constant contact with each other for however long our race survives.

There is no climactic ending to this story. There were no deaths. There were no massive changes in the world, and everything was more or less the same when I got back to Missouri. This story would have been much easier to write if there had been some big climax when I turned into my parents' driveway, but there wasn't. I was a little different, sure. I had more stories and I had longer hair. Other than that, this story just ends. Worlds end in whispers, not bangs, and the same is true for memoirs. Climactic endings are for fiction and those who go out in a blaze of glory. Most of us are not fortunate enough to burn so bright.

Like everyone else who ends an adventure alive, the story just keeps going. I don't know what I expected when I turned into the driveway. My family and extended family were there to greet me with open arms, bright smiles, and grilled meat.

One of the things my dad joked about several times before I left when I talked about growing a beard and going off into the woods to get lost while on the trip was that I was going to turn into a lumbersexual. At the gas station a couple blocks away from their house, I changed out of my shorts and put on jeans, a flannel, and hung an ax in my belt. When I pulled into the driveway full of cars and smoke from the grill, the first thing I yelled to my dad as he walked out of the house was that his lumbersexual son had returned.

We hugged, cried, joked, and played games for the rest of the day until everyone eventually went home. I sat outside under the night sky just a little longer than the rest before going upstairs to the room I grew up in.

Nietzsche wrote about eternal recurrence: the idea that we are destined to live the same lives the same way ad infinitum. Every choice, every breath, every leap of faith, every success, and every failure we are doomed or blessed to repeat in the exact same way for an eternity to come.

But within these connected rings of infinite, repeated lives, is what I think of as eternal occurrence. Something is always happening: there is no such thing as total stillness, no such thing as being motionless. There is no findable beginning, and it does not look like there will ever be an end. After all the big, transformative moments and all our adventures, whether they are major injuries, road trips, skydiving, marriage, having children, going to college, whatever the moments bring, something is always next. Even death. Bodily death is just what must happen before we get to an even grander adventure. We are not blessed with multiple endings. We could not be so fortunate as to end one book and reach for another multiple times. All we can do is love every word we read before turning the page to see what happens next.

So, this is it. This is the ending of the chapter and the story.

In a couple weeks, I have to start packing for college, and then I'll move out again and into the next thing that will occur. I have to unpack the van at some point, too, but I want to hold off on that if I can. I might sleep in it a few more times before driving it back to my grandparents. I might sit in the captain's chair in the driveway with my hands on the wheel and close my eyes to see the mountains, the canyons, the deserts, and the forests unfold before me. I might turn around and see all the people I met along the way crammed into the van with beaming smiles on their faces, ready for the next adventure.

Part III

The Photographic Journey

4. A Rocky Start

5. Strangers

6. The Blizzard and the Sun Devil

7. Somewhere East of Jesus

9. Adam in the Garden of Eden

10. Up and Down the Mountain

11. Tomorrow May Never Happen, Yesterday Will Never Happen Again

12. Sea to Sky

13. Icefields Parkway

14. Glacier

15. Coming Down from the High

Made in the USA
Columbia, SC
16 November 2021

48531349R00115